It's the Mission, Not the Mandates

It's the Mission, Not the Mandates

Defining the Purpose of Public Education

Amy Fast

ROWMAN & LITTLEFIELD
Lanham • Boulder • New York • London

Published by Rowman & Littlefield
A wholly owned subsidiary of The Rowman & Littlefield Publishing Group, Inc.
4501 Forbes Boulevard, Suite 200, Lanham, Maryland 20706
www.rowman.com

Unit A, Whitacre Mews, 26-34 Stannary Street, London SE11 4AB

Copyright © 2016 by Amy Fast

All rights reserved. No part of this book may be reproduced in any form or by any electronic or mechanical means, including information storage and retrieval systems, without written permission from the publisher, except by a reviewer who may quote passages in a review.

British Library Cataloguing in Publication Information Available

Library of Congress Cataloging-in-Publication Data

Names: Fast, Amy.
Title: It's the mission, not the mandates : defining the purpose of public education / Amy Fast.
Description: Lanham, Maryland : Rowman & Littlefield, [2015] | Includes bibliographical references.
Identifiers: LCCN 2015026468 | ISBN 9781475823356 (cloth : alk. paper) | ISBN 9781475823363 (pbk. : alk. paper) | ISBN 9781475823370 (electronic)
Subjects: LCSH: Public schools—United States. | Education—United States. | Education—Aims and objectives—United States. | Educational Evaluation—United States.
Classification: LCC LA217.2 .F37 2015 | DDC 371.010973—dc23 LC record available at http://lccn.loc.gov/2015026468

∞™ The paper used in this publication meets the minimum requirements of American National Standard for Information Sciences—Permanence of Paper for Printed Library Materials, ANSI/NISO Z39.48-1992.

Printed in the United States of America

Contents

Preface		vii
The Ache for Meaning		vii
1	The Need for Purpose	1
	Education and a Sense of Purpose	7
2	Our Past Priorities	17
	The Colonial Period	17
	American Education in the Nineteenth Century	19
	Progressive Period	21
	Post-Progressive Era and the Conservative Movement	23
	The Pendulum Swings of American Educational Philosophy	27
3	Our Current Priorities	31
	College and Career Ready	31
	Teacher Effectiveness	40
	Assessment and Measurement	43
	Back to the Basics	46
4	Society's Needs and Values	55
	Civic Needs	57
	Economic Needs	59
	Social Needs	61
	What the Public Wants	72
5	Finding a Noble Purpose	83
	A Purpose That Inspires	83
	Out with Reform and in with Revolution	86
	Assessment and Accountability	92

	Creating the Village	96
	Implications for the Curriculum	101
	Implications for Instruction	108
	Implications for Society	115
6	Conclusion	119
Appendix		125
Bibliography		127
About the Author		137

Preface

THE ACHE FOR MEANING

"It's all about what's best for kids," the principal recited with a strained smile as he tracked the numbers across the page with his finger. This phrase had become the motto of educational leaders in our country, and at face value it sounded rather noble. The only problem was that the phrase always seemed to preclude a mandate that, while good intentioned, rarely felt best for our students in practice.

"So . . . what are we at here? Seventy-eight percent? That's not bad at all for round two. And, David didn't pass, did he? Right there we have a chance to bring your class up to eighty-one percent." His eyes suddenly widened with hope as he kicked off the carpet gliding his chair smoothly over to his file cabinet. The principal pulled open a drawer and held up a bag of peppermints triumphantly. "Did you give them the mints?"

Peppermints. Peppermints were his obsession around testing time. Somewhere, years ago, he had read that sucking on them helped students to focus and ever since, he regarded the peppermint as the silver bullet of student achievement. In some desperate attempt to give the data a boost when good old-fashioned teaching and learning were proving to be too tedious and complex, the peppermint would save the day. I had to stifle a chuckle given the irony.

What's best for kids, huh? Pushing 160 pounds in the fourth grade, peppermints certainly did not come to mind when reflecting on what was best for David. "I don't know," I replied. "I think his score is a pretty good reflection of where he is in his reading development. I mean, of course it is only March, so he's still going to make quite a bit of progress before the end of the year. If we take another two weeks to test him a third time, he is going to miss out on so much reading instruction. Plus, I've recently met with his parents, and I'm really excited. We spent a good hour last week creating a plan they can work on as a family over the summer to make sure that he continues to grow as a reader and can maybe even learn to love reading by next September! Surprisingly, David even sounded like he could get on board! It's a really great idea actually."

"If we can get your class up to eighty-one percent," the principal cut me off, "the fourth grade would be at seventy-four percent overall. I think this could keep us out of the red." "The red" referred to a color-coded chart that was handed out each fall at the beginning of the school year and indicated whether each grade and each school in the district was above or below state average in the tested subjects.

This was *the* barometer of success in our district and where the buck stopped. The infamous chart dictated which schools were working, which schools were "failing," which principals would be retained, and which principals would be transferred to less desirable roles. I deflated a bit as I realized that this man was grasping for green, and all bets were placed on me in hopes of achieving it this year.

It's not that I didn't like the vote of confidence because secretly I reveled in the fact that it gave me some clout in this game. What bothered me was that if it was really about "what was best for kids" then my colleague in the fourth grade would have been called in to speak with our boss as well. I had just talked to her earlier in the staff room, and she was telling me how many struggling students she had this year and how she was really feeling alone in trying to meet their needs.

Yet, here I was because I was known throughout the intermediate team as a teacher who got results, so the fact that I was the most likely means of improving our ranking on our standardized test scores made practical sense, and I would likely even embrace the idea if it made ethical sense as well. But, therein lay the problem.

For years we had given our attention and interventions to students who would have the highest probability of meeting the cut score on the state test. This meant that we dumped our time and resources into the "bubble kids" (the students who were not too far off from passing) often at the expense of the most struggling learners. This also meant that we put all our stock in our effective teachers and too frequently turned a blind eye to those on whom we had given up hope or on those who were too involved in the union to risk chancing a difficult conversation.

In addition, we were told that we could not waste any time discussing or attempting to find solutions for obstacles that were "out of our control," including parent involvement, students' safety and nurturing outside of the school walls, and basically any other needs that did not have an overtly direct connection to that which we measured and were measured by.

I felt for my boss. I really did. I could see that he was also facing overwhelming pressure himself, and he hadn't even been able to come up for air in the past ten years—much less stop to reflect on whether or not *he* even bought into that which he was selling. His reputation, his pride, and his job were on the line, and he was simply doing what he was told by those who better understood the policies and the intentions behind them. Surely, he thought that with which he was tasked was what was best for his school and his students.

So, his time was spent hanging onto "the green" by his fingernails in order to feel like he mattered in this business of helping students, as that was the measure. If he kept his eye on that prize, he hoped he would be making a difference by maintaining the "laser-like focus" that schools across America were being begged to employ. He knew that focus was shown to be *the* variable that set apart high-performing schools from their failing counterparts. All educators had heard of Reeves' (2003) research as it was driving much education reform in the country.

Doug Reeves, in his famous 90-90-90 study, examined American schools that had at least 90 percent students from poverty, at least 90 percent students of minority status, and at least 90 percent of students meeting the standards. These schools defied the odds and were statistical anomalies, so Reeves wanted to discover the variables that set them apart in hopes that if we could emulate those variables in public schools across America, maybe other schools would see similar results.

It turned out that all of the 90-90-90 schools shared a handful of characteristics, including an emphasis on nonfiction writing, clear curriculum choices, common and frequent assessments to gauge learning, collaborative scoring of student work, and most importantly, a "laser-like focus" on academic achievement. It was no wonder teachers and principals in our district were being asked to push everything else aside in favor of intense attention to the results. After all, we owed it to our students to be intentional about how we spent our time with them and emphasize in the classroom that which would provide them with the most leverage for success later in life.

No one had been a bigger proponent of this laser-like focus than me. Leaders in education were not wrong to suggest that it was time to raise our expectations for students and to treat every second in schools as the precious moment needed to provide opportunity to children that it was. Educational leaders were not wrong to suspect that we could do better in classrooms across America.

Of course, we could. It was time to get on the same page in education instead of operating like independent contractors, and it was time to believe in our students. In fact, I had even given a speech a few years back at our district's "welcome back" ceremonies at the start of the new school year in which I pleaded with school staff to come together and raise our expectations of students and to never label a child as someone who cannot succeed. The tide of education in America was changing, and I wanted to be one of the first to hop on the wave of hope and high expectations.

The problem began to emerge, however, when that laser-like focus in our country began to function a little more like tunnel vision. Slowly, the results began to supersede the learning itself. If a student scored well by virtue of probability on multiple-choice assessment items and the score did not reflect the student's actual struggle in the subject area, we considered it a success.

Conversely, if a student was demonstrating advanced critical thinking skills and was a motivated learner with a vision of who he wanted to be in life but by some fluke did not pass the end-of-year assessment, we considered it a failure. This obsessive focus on results confused our purpose as educators, as it put competition and numbers ahead of student need, and the subsequent scramble to understand and play the ever bewildering numbers game left us *all* hanging by our fingernails.

We were so busy hanging on that no one ever stopped to ask why. Why exactly did we come here every day? What was our real purpose . . . beyond making our school and our district *look* successful to the powers that be? What *was* best for our students? Although we understood the connection between academic achievement and opportunity, we rarely discussed it. And, outside that connection, we knew in our guts that we were charged with the monumental responsibility of growing humans, and success on that undertaking hinged on so much more than just academic achievement.

How did we get ourselves into this game where we had somehow won if we reached the right number of students who proved proficient at their basic reading and math skills yet were not able to demonstrate responsibility and respect . . . and lose if we did not meet that magic number but quite literally saved some students' lives by inspiring them to believe in themselves and pursue their passions?

That elusive, noble purpose was at best something that each educator had to articulate and define for herself each day in order to continue to make decisions in the best interest of students. At worst, it remained a mystery or was lost in the endless stream of mandates and measures. One thing was certain, however. That lost purpose was the light at the end of the tunnel for which we all yearned.

Of course we were here to educate these kids, but to what end? It seemed that the only end to which everyone was being pointed was better scores on our standardized tests, but that was certainly not what inspired us to get out of bed every morning and whispered to our hearts every day. We were in this profession to improve lives, not just numbers. Yet, somewhere along the line we started focusing so much on the measure that we lost sight of the mission.

The purpose of this book is to argue the need to establish a nobler mission for America's schools and to propose that doing so could both motivate and mold the very public that public education serves. French aviator and author, Antoine de Saint-Exupery, once said that "if you want to build a ship, don't drum up people together to collect wood and don't assign them tasks and work, but rather teach them to long for the endless immensity of the sea."

Throughout this text, I will argue that we have lost our way in public education in America—that we are spending so much time figuring out how to build a quality ship that we have lost sight of the sea. I will argue that now, more than ever, in this era where the means has become more important than the end, educators ache for a more inspiring mission than simply improving student outcome on standardized assessments.

I will illustrate how focusing on the mission instead of simply the mandates and measures is how real change occurs, and I will attempt to uncover a more motivating and meaningful purpose for public education and illustrate how that purpose—that longing for the sea—will ultimately inspire stakeholders of public education and will lead to real change rather than short-sighted reform.

Ultimately, I hope to persuade stakeholders that if American schools really are agents for societal change, then we need to reassess our greatest needs and values as a society and make sure that our end goals in public education are aligned with those ideals. Until our purpose of public education addresses the real needs of society, stakeholders of public education will likely continue to spend their time quarreling over the various initiatives that fall off the pendulum of reform as it swings back and forth.

Similar to what educators refer to as the "backwards design model," or starting with the objectives of what we hope to accomplish with students before moving on to a plan for how to meet those objectives, we too, as the *public* that public education is charged with serving, need to define for ourselves our own objectives for what we hope schools accomplish before rolling out various reforms on how we are going to get there.

As a current educator in public education, my perspective is unique in that I am still "in the trenches," for lack of a better phrase. While many authors on education write from a perspective that is often more removed from the classroom, I have the unique lens of a practitioner who is still working in schools. I work daily as an instructional coach to improve teaching and increase learning in schools, and yet I am also immersed daily in the unintended consequences of trying to improve instruction and achievement before engaging in the larger discussion about what we want most for our students and our society.

I have witnessed the burnout and frustration of school leaders who wonder why these teachers just "won't get on board." I have felt firsthand the systematic demoralization of teachers who, day in and day out, try their hardest to do what is best for students, only to be told they are failing by measures that seem arbitrary. And, I have seen the smiles disappear off students' faces as they sit through what seems like pointless instruction that does not feel relevant to their lives or their futures. I do not wish, however, to place blame.

Leaders are working tirelessly to carry out initiatives they are told will change the trajectory of students' lives and our communities' well-being. Teachers are tapping into their emotional reserves for the last remains of selflessness and passion they can muster to somehow implement the barrage of new federal and state mandates while simultaneously trying to keep their students' best interest in mind. I truly believe that stakeholders of public education in America are mostly well intentioned. The problem as I see it is that we have failed to engage in a much needed discussion about our greatest purpose.

I believe wholeheartedly that this conversation—if it is happening—needs to include all the voices of the "public," for whom public education exists, and if it is not happening, it is long overdue. It's a simple question: What *is* the greatest mission of our schools? And, yet, landing on an answer is no simple feat.

Chapter 1

The Need for Purpose

The success of any organization hinges upon the drive of its members. Equally important to that success is that those individuals are all "driving" in the same direction. Business leaders used to believe that employees' motivation and the subsequent success of the organization in which they worked boiled down to a simple formula of rewards and punishment. The idea was that the more money one earned, the more productive the worker.

Simultaneously, the harder the hammer dropped on lazy or ineffective workers, the more likely they would be to step up their efforts and improve their abilities. In other words, the key to productivity was thought to be extrinsic motivation. In fact, for a long time much research even backed up this idea that motivation boiled down simply to what was in it for the employees.

However, as jobs changed to meet the demands of the twenty-first century, what motivated employees changed as well. Whereas the jobs of old simply required basic direction-following and mundane, repetitive duties, twenty-first-century careers require more critical thinking, problem solving, and imagination—assets that cannot be elicited from employees with "carrot and stick" strategies.

Carrot and stick strategies refer to financial incentives such as salaries and bonuses and punitive incentives such as deadlines, schedules, and disciplinary action. These tactics, research has revealed, only work when the goal is compliance. Compliance, however, can only get a company so far. Employees who are striving to simply be compliant often only put in the minimal amount of work required to fulfill their job descriptions. No one ever cited compliance as the factor that made millions or changed the world.

Perhaps the most famous study attributed with changing the conversation on employee motivation is McGregor's 1960 Theory X and Theory Y research. In his research, McGregor identified that there are two basic models of organizational management, and only one of them—Theory X—is founded on compliance. Employers who adopt the Theory X model assume that most people do not like work, and for this reason they need to be controlled in order to do the job and do it well.

However, McGregor offers an alternative to this kind of leadership with his Theory Y model. Under Theory Y, the assumption is that work is as natural and fulfilling of a human desire as play or rest and that if a person is committed to the overall goal of his organization, he will be self-motivated and, thus, there will be very little need to control him through rewards and punishment. Finally, McGregor asserts that if Theory Y is not utilized then we are not tapping into employees' full intellectual potential.

Recently, Daniel Pink (2011) expanded on McGregor's research asserting that intrinsic motivation (referred to by McGregor as Theory Y) is the key to organizational success because success in the twenty-first century is not founded on compliance but rather on the internal drive of each individual. He breaks motivation down even further by defining three basic will-drivers that inspire and fuel all individuals and, in turn, move companies forward: autonomy, mastery, and purpose.

When these three motivators are all present within an organization, success is optimized as employees are encouraged to utilize their unique strengths, are confident in their abilities, and are inspired by the shared mission. Autonomy refers to the amount of freedom and individuality that employers nurture in their organizations. When employees feel trusted to figure out how to best carry out the work, they are more likely to work harder and more effectively.

Moreover, when employees feel valued for their unique strengths that they bring to the table, they feel that their contributions matter, so their drive to do well increases (Pink 2011). Likewise, they naturally want to do well at that with which they are tasked. When workers feel good at what they do—when they have achieved mastery at a complex task or skill—they enjoy their work and feel that they have much to offer the organization. People who enjoy their work and do it well often define the state in which they do their work as this intangible feeling of "flow" (Csikszentmihalyi 2000).

Flow is a state in which the work seems almost effortless, and yet the one experiencing the feeling of flow is at a heightened level of efficiency and effectiveness, described by many who experience it as an almost out-of-body experience. Many athletes cite being in this state of flow when they break records or achieve unprecedented results. This flow—or this mind-set of optimal engagement through mastery—is another one of the factors that Pink says propels individuals and organizations forward.

Finally, the third and possibly most important motivator for individuals in twenty-first-century careers is a strong sense of purpose. "The most deeply motivated people," Pink (2011) states, "—not to mention those who are most productive and satisfied—hitch their desires to a cause larger than themselves" (p. 131). In fact, successful businesses around the world are finding out that more imperative to success than the profit motive is the "purpose motive."

The companies that are surpassing others in this global economy are often the companies that stand for something other than just making money—those that have the greater mission of contributing something to the world. This is because people crave meaning in their work as well as their lives. It turns out that if you hire people based on their abilities to do a job, they will work for the sake of making a living, but if you hire people whose beliefs are congruent with the greater mission of the work, they will give you their blood, sweat, and tears (Sinek 2009).

Other researchers echo this claim that purpose should be at the forefront of our work. Dan Ariely (2008), professor of psychology at Duke University, discusses marketplace motivators (carrot and stick strategies) versus social motivators (autonomy, mastery, and purpose) at the workplace and cites various social experiments to illustrate his point that social motivators evoke much more passion and commitment than marketplace motivators.

One particular experiment described by Ariely illustrates the effect of purpose on motivation. In the study, researchers had participants follow directions to put an object together with Legos. In the experiment there were those who admittedly loved putting together Legos and those who were not as fond of playing with them.

Initially, using financial incentives, they found what many studies prior had found—that interestingly, zero payment had more effect on motivation to complete the task and efficiency of completing the task than low payment and that high payment also had more effect than low payment. In other words, getting paid well or simply doing something for pleasure (or because one is being counted on to do it) is more motivating than being paid less than one is worth.

However, another variable was then added to the experiment. This time, immediately after the participant put together the Legos, the researchers had someone take them apart right in front of that individual—essentially taking away any purpose in the task whatsoever. With this variable added, productivity and motivation dropped significantly, and this remained true regardless of how much the participant was paid. In other words, a lack of purpose made financial rewards virtually ineffective.

It did not matter if participants were paid the higher amount because the lack of purpose demotivated them to the point that they lost their drive and efficiency. Purpose, Ariely asserts, is *the* difference between motivation and demoralization. Placing *why* at the center of whatever industry we are in allows us to achieve beyond our assumptions of what is possible.

In a recent 2009 study, Simon Sinek, an expert on organizational leadership and advisor on matters of military innovation and development, codified the language used by individuals and organizations whose accomplishments had far exceeded the status quo. He found that a pattern emerged in the way successful individuals and groups communicated. Moreover, the similarities that emerged were in stark contrast to how others in similar fields who did not achieve success communicated.

People who put the "why" of their work at the center of their thoughts, actions, and words were able to move others to join in their mission and to tap into others' full potential in order to maximize success. On the other hand, people who addressed the "why" of their work as an afterthought or not at all employed individuals who stopped at simply fulfilling their assigned duties.

The "why" of an organization can be thought of as its cause, belief, or purpose. Organizations like Apple, says Sinek (2009), who start with the why and then move to the how and what, know that people do not buy what companies *do*, but rather *why* they do it. Sinek states that there are numerous computer companies that exist but none are as successful as Apple even though many competing companies create products equal in quality to Apple's products.

In other computer companies' advertising, he illustrates, they highlight their product, explain how it works or how it can benefit the consumer, and then *maybe* allude to what the company stands for on a deeper level. Apple, however, starts by communicating its belief that everything it does should challenge the status quo and stem from thinking outside the box.

This belief is communicated to consumers of Apple products through their actions and words, and time and again people invest in Apple products, not because they know a lot about the product itself but because they are excited by the notion of innovation and pushing the envelope of the status quo.

Surprisingly, though, very few organizations keep the "why" at the center of their work. The reason, Sinek (2009) explains, is because the "what" is so much easier and clearer to define and explain. So, it is natural to go from the most tangible aspect of our work to the most intangible instead of the other way around. However, he argues that companies should make a concerted effort to do so because this idea of purpose as a motivator is not only in our business plans but in our biology as well.

When we are being sold a product or service by being shown what the product is, what it can do, how it works, etc., the part of our brain that responds—the neocortex—is the same part of our brain that is responsible for comprehending complex information and using logic. On the other hand, when we are being sold a product or service by connecting with a deeply held system of beliefs or a vision for new possibilities, then our limbic brain—the part of our brain that experiences emotion and is used to make decisions—is activated. It is in the limbic brain where our motivation is cultivated (Sinek 2009).

Sinek (2009) uses the example of Martin Luther King Jr.'s (MLK) ability to move the masses during the civil rights era to illustrate the power of purpose. Although it seems unlikely for one man to inspire such change, he and others in history have done just that. MLK was able to create positive and substantial change in our country, not because he was able to articulate *what* should change and roll out a plan for *how* to make the change but because he was able to inspire others with his vision of equality for all.

Sinek (2009) asserts that there are leaders and there are those who lead, and the difference lies with one's ability to inspire others with a cause that moves them. After all, he states, "MLK gave the 'I have a dream' speech, not the 'I have a plan' speech" (17:06).

Yet, organizations spend countless hours addressing what work needs to get done and how to do the work, and employees rarely understand the deeper reasons behind why they are doing it. Even businesses that do not seem to have a valiant mission on the surface can and should foster a noble purpose. Rather than a jewelry designer thinking that her purpose is to sell accessories to make a profit, what if she thought of her role as helping others to feel their best by expressing themselves through their attire?

Instead of a travel agent thinking of his purpose as racking up as many clients as he can and making a profit off of their exotic vacations, what if he thought of his role as helping others to find the relaxation that they need and deserve or as helping others to experience unique places and cultures so that they can become more open minded and well rounded? Simply putting an emphasis on the greater purpose activates the passion and meaning in our careers for which we yearn.

If people did understand that most noble purpose in whatever field they worked, their thirst for meaning could be quenched, and they would be inspired to find the most effective and efficient ways to actually do the work. Without understanding the organization's purpose, however, the work becomes more of a chore than a calling, and therefore, innovation and passion are replaced with compliance and demoralization.

While simply fostering a sense of purpose will propel organizations forward, articulating a purpose that has service to others at its core has the potential to move mountains. It turns out that not only are workers happier and more motivated when they feel that their professional endeavors are meaningful, but consumers and clients of organizations respond more to the organization's purpose than its products, as well.

Economic growth in the twenty-first century is dependent upon businesses who define their roles beyond the products they sell or the services they offer. Keeping purpose at the forefront of the mission cultivates intrinsic motivation of the organization's employees. Likewise, when companies emphasize how they serve the communities that sustain them, consumers are motivated, as well.

Companies such as TOMS, whose mission is to improve people's lives by donating a pair of shoes to someone in need every time a pair is purchased should not be profitable based on old financial market values. However, because they operate with a purpose of service as the driving force of the company rather than the bottom line, they break the mold when it comes to successful business models that not only make large margins of profit but are also changing the world by igniting employees' and customers' senses of purpose (Pink 2011).

When people have a purpose beyond just making a profit, they are moved intrinsically, and that collective drive thrusts the organization forward. When this happens, the profit becomes the means by which they achieve the end rather than the end goal itself. Money, it turns out after all, is not our prime motivator because there is little correlation between what we make and how happy we are.

While money does have a strong correlation with one's subjective well-being, it does not have a strong correlation with one's positive or negative feelings or demeanor. Happiness, rather, has a stronger correlation with our psychological needs than our economic status. Although many of us assume otherwise, our happiness is dependent more on our sense of purpose than on the contents of our pocketbook.

Leipzig (2014) found that, surprisingly, what many of us consider to be the constructs of success, such as money, healthy relationships, a promising career, and so on were not, in fact, indicators of happiness among successful adults. Of the successful individuals he interviewed, many more stated that they were unhappy than those who stated that they were happy.

This finding seemed to be counterintuitive as those whom Leipzig interviewed had accomplished and attained much of what most Americans seem to desire from life. However, when further probing the small group of successful individuals who stated that they were actually happy, Leipzig found that they all had one commonality: they knew their life purpose.

He discovered that regardless of the lives they led or the industries in which they worked, these people were able to articulate how their work helped others. The difference between the unhappy individuals and those who were happy was that the unhappy individuals continued to chase happiness by looking inward in order to determine how to help themselves, whereas happy individuals kept their focus outward on how they could help others.

While having a noble purpose is imperative to having happy and motivated employees, common sense tells us that if each employee in an organization is operating under a different purpose than his colleagues, the full potential of each individual might be optimized, but realizing the potential of the entire organization is less likely to happen. If each member of the organization is driven but is driving in different directions, organizational chaos will ensue. Thus, it is also essential that the organization's purpose is both noble and transparent to all stakeholders.

EDUCATION AND A SENSE OF PURPOSE

If purpose is such an integral part of successful organizations and individuals, then organizations and individuals who are crucial to the betterment of society need to be even more cognizant of keeping a noble purpose at the heart of their work. It is not an exaggeration to say that those in the field of public education are in the business of changing the world. And because educators are humanitarians at heart, although mastery and autonomy undoubtedly play a role in their drive to do better, purpose is arguably the prominent will-driver of most in the profession.

A strong sense of purpose is likely what drew most educators to their work in the first place. When you ask teachers why they wanted to become educators, their response is almost always that which illustrates a strong desire to help children. They might respond that they love working with kids or that they feel fulfilled when they experience that "light bulb moment" in their classes when a student finally gains a new understanding.

Oftentimes, educators state that they know that children are the key to improving society—that they are the future of our communities—and that there is no work more important than investing in that future. Regardless of how educators answer the question, you can bet that they can articulate why it is that they get into the profession. Maintaining that sense of purpose is vital to maintaining educators' drive and focus on the tasks most crucial to realizing that vision.

It might seem fruitless then if educators' initial purpose in entering the profession rolls off their tongues with such ease to examine whether or not public education in America has a clearly articulated purpose through which those invested in our schools can find inspiration. However, if one were to ask a student, parent, business leader, educator, administrator, or politician to define public education's greatest purpose, the responses would likely vary . . . *if* stakeholders were able to give clear and concise responses at all.

Some stakeholders may describe the need to create responsible and active democratic citizens to ensure that our country continues to nurture the ideals of freedom and equality. Some may discuss the importance of preparing students for the global economy so that America can maintain its competitive edge. Or possibly those invested in public education might discuss the woes of today's communities, the downfalls of our society, and the need to instill better moral compasses in our children by teaching social skills, self-monitoring strategies, responsibility to the greater good, and a respect for authority.

There are also those who will state that we can serve students best by encouraging them to pursue their passions, allowing them to explore that which interests them most, and letting them grow at their own pace in order to foster a love for learning. Finally, many stakeholders are likely to state all or a combination of all of these ideals as our greatest goals in public education.

In 2011, the Association for Educational Communication and Technology (AECT) did extensive research on what scholars and experts in the field of education viewed as public education's greatest purposes. They gathered educational leaders together and asked them what our greatest purposes in education should be. While some broad themes did emerge, such as being a citizen of the country and workforce preparation, the conversation was extremely hard to codify and use as a basis for determining a common vision because inevitably the conversation about purpose always went to obstacles and solutions instead.

This illustrates what is likely happening on a larger, national level as well. If even those who are experts in education have a hard time articulating and landing on a common purpose, imagine how difficult it is for citizens and politicians who are invested in the matter but do not possess the depth of knowledge on the subject that scholars in the field of education do.

Thus, what ends up happening time and again is that rather than beginning with the end in mind—rather than starting with this kind of analysis as a national conversation about public education—what tends to happen is that our conversation about public education in America jumps to calls for immediate action and quick fixes. While having a sense of urgency to better our public education system for our children is certainly a good thing, sprinting off in various directions before we understand where we are intending to go is quite another.

The AECT suggests that, rather, we should begin with a rigorous needs assessment on our country and its schools in order to serve as a meaningful foundation for the conversation on school reform. If identifying a shared purpose is that challenging for educational experts, imagine the difficulty that the public has—the very group that *public* education is designed to serve.

In 2001, in conducting a report for the Joint Legislative Committee to develop a master plan for education, the California Research Bureau interviewed various stakeholders in public education to determine the sheer breadth of purposes desired from public education. What they found was that all issues vexing society become the issues we expect public education to fix; if there is a problem the public wants addressed, we throw it into the pot.

Purposes that emerged from their study included providing students with multiple opportunities for success, creating good democratic citizens, fostering academic success for all, preparing students for postsecondary education, preparing students for the workforce, passing down the values of American society, fostering personal growth, creating life-long learners, providing opportunity for life, liberty, and the pursuit of happiness for all, ensuring basic competencies in reading, writing, and arithmetic, providing free child care, developing a child's self-esteem and good work habits, teaching life skills, combating the effects of bad parenting, preparing students to compete in the global economy, nurturing creativity and imagination, developing individuality, promoting good health, providing vocational preparation, preparing students for life and leisure, separating and selecting students for the American elite, promoting a peaceful society, promoting a prosperous society, and promoting a moral society. And, that list is not exhaustive (de Cos 2001).

With so many goals, is it even possible to land on a shared mission in public education? Arguably, no matter how many purposes something has, a greater, overarching purpose always exists. Regardless of the challenge that determining a common purpose presents, the need is urgent and immense. Many scholars have argued that in addition to the *why* of public education needing to be defined, the *what* and *how* are struggling as well.

Simply creating a congruent curriculum that is vertically aligned from prekindergarten to twelfth grade (the *what*) has been quite the chore, and even though most states are implementing the Common Core State Standards in an attempt to create this congruence, many educators are not implementing those standards with fidelity once their classroom doors are shut.

Furthermore, even though many districts across the country are attempting to identify a shared understanding of what good teaching looks like (the *how*), professional development and evaluation have not changed enough to realize this common understanding and make a real difference in classrooms. One reason may be that we continue to put our money and efforts into the *what* and *how* of public education before we have a clear understanding of the *why*.

One reason there is so much ambiguity and confusion about public education's greatest purpose—the *why*—is because so many essential purposes exist simultaneously. But, to further complicate the matter, although there is so much that is desired and expected from public education, many of these hopes for what our schools accomplish rarely get measured, rarely get our resources, or, therefore, rarely get our focus.

And, if that isn't frustrating enough for those in the trenches of the work, many have expressed concern that what we *do* measure (usually through standardized assessments) is not even capturing the learning that policymakers and the tests they roll out intend. So, while it is frequently stated that what gets tested gets taught, we should be concerned not only with whether our assessments reflect our greatest purposes but also whether our assessments accurately reflect the learning and gains that they are supposed to measure.

We are constantly collecting data, whether they are data from our standardized state (now national) assessments, data from our local formative assessments, or data from global institutes that compare the achievement of different countries. Findings from the data gleaned from these assessments are then used to inform policy. However, Beista (2009) argues that we are analyzing the facts without contextualizing them in our values saying that the "targets and indicators of quality become mistaken for quality itself" (p. 35).

If the tests do not measure what we value, and yet the tests determine what we teach, then it is probable that we are not even teaching what we value most. In a recent study, West, Gabrieli, Finn, Kraft, and Gabrieli (2014) found that schools are often able to increase test scores without increasing students' critical-thinking skills. However, because testing has become the end goal rather than simply a measure, we often do not concern ourselves with students' actual learning and growth so long as they are measuring up on the tests.

When there is so much pressure on achieving results on standardized assessments, and yet our assessments do not always match the kinds of thinking and skills that we know provide students with the most opportunity for success in life, it places us in an ethical dilemma. Diane Ravitch (2011), who once participated in think tanks that eventually pushed high stakes testing legislation forward but has since changed her stance on education reform, goes even further to imply that there is no noble purpose whatsoever in current education policy.

She audaciously asserts that current education policy has less to do with a service-based purpose and more to do with the money and power that will be gained by those promoting the agenda. No wonder educators often feel confused and uninspired by their purpose. Many educators are not only uninspired by the current culture of education, but they are also worried that the very purpose behind current education reform was not born from moral intentions.

> What was once the standards movement was replaced by the accountability movement. What once was an effort to improve the quality of education turned into an accounting strategy: measure, then punish or reward. No education experience was needed to administer such a program. Anyone who loved data could do it. The strategy produced fear and obedience among educators; it often generated higher test scores. But it had nothing to do with education (Ravitch 2011, p. 16).

This inner battle of struggling to believe that what educators are being mandated to implement is actually what is best for our students often pushes teachers from compliance to defiance. Ironically, on top of this defiance, the lack of a shared and noble vision brings about the lack of focus—the same focus that the 90-90-90 study determined was imperative to gains in academic achievement.

While it could be true that increased accountability and a more coherent curriculum are necessary in schools, we will never fully realize the benefits of these reforms if we do not get teachers on board. If teachers are not on board, many will likely continue to just sit silent in an assumed agreement as the reforms are rolled out but shut the doors to their classroom and do their own thing when no one is watching. We cannot blame them either. If they do not understand the purpose behind these initiatives, or worse, if they assume that the purpose behind the initiatives is not ethical, then what motivation do they have to be compliant, much less fully committed?

One reason that teachers struggle to carry out the mandate for increased standardized testing results is because the greatest needs that they see students bringing to their classrooms are not always academic. And while academics are obviously the primary task with which schools are charged, future success of students hinges on much more than academic skill.

Most of us would argue that successful, happy people possess much more than just academic prowess. Thus, teachers struggle to employ a curriculum that consists mostly of test preparation when many of their students are void of the basic social and intrapersonal skills—referred to often as "soft skills"—necessary to make it in life.

In a short speech on what students need most from their education, Howard Gardner (2014), the Harvard professor attributed with the groundbreaking research on Multiple Intelligences, discussed the current emphasis on wit and grit in schools. Gardner stated that there are limits to solely focusing on students' cognitive skills (wit) and their ability to push through and stick with challenges (grit).

After all, he reminded his audience, Nazi soldiers had grit. The CEOs of Enron had wit. There are more elements necessary to produce good people, good workers, and good citizens, which he refers to as "the triple helix." Gardner asserts that if we are really hoping to create *good* people, workers, and citizens, then we need to focus on excellence, engagement, *and* ethics. After all, Gardner (2014) states, isn't our hope that we use our intelligence to actually make a difference in the world?

Daniel Goleman, the leading expert on emotional intelligence (2012), also provides research that validates teachers' gut feelings that there is more to education than just academic achievement. In his extensive research on the characteristics of effective leadership, Goleman found that a leader's emotional intelligence is *twice* as effective as his cognitive and technical ability *combined*.

In other words, the leaders who are able to affect the most change in their organizations exhibit greater ability to empathize, self-regulate, and utilize exemplary social skills. If these traits are so crucial to leaders' success, then they are likely to be crucial to the members of their workforce as well. If emotional intelligence carries so much weight in affecting change—more so than cognitive ability and technical ability—then wouldn't we want to ensure that students gain emotional intelligence as part of their preparation for the "real world," as well?

However, there are no standards or measures for emotional intelligence or ethics even though both Gardner and Goleman assure us that not only can they be learned, but they are crucial to students' future success as well. The assumption by policymakers and by those making the decisions in districts around the country must be that these factors are taken care of outside of school, are already present prior to students entering school, or are impossible to address in our schools. If these are not, in fact, assumptions of our leaders, then the only possibility left is to assume that future success and happiness are not large priorities to educational leaders.

When teachers try to explain to administrators that there are skills and knowledge that are equally important for students beyond information necessary to do well on standardized tests, they are often accused of making excuses to avoid the hard task of helping all students to achieve proficiency on the standards. Teachers then feel as though they are not being heard, and some silently rebel while others relentlessly fight against the system.

This dynamic has led some to label educators as "whiners" and has become prevalent in our society today. In fact, recently teachers have been vilified by the very communities that they serve. The rhetoric that American schools are failing our students has continually increased over the past thirty years, and teachers are not deaf to this discussion. Many make teachers scapegoats for the failings of public education stating that they are largely ineffective and unaccountable for what they do in their classrooms.

While there may be merit to the argument that we need to tighten our systems of accountability in schools, there is likely also merit to the concerns of teachers. After all, what is more probable, that the majority of teachers by nature are lazy whiners who avoid responsibility or that there is actually something that happens to teachers once they are immersed in their careers that is, in fact, justifiably frustrating and not working for students?

Yet, while the rest of the world embraces this idea of purpose as fuel for intrinsic motivation and organizational success (the Theory Y model), public education seems to be gripping tighter and tighter to the principles of Theory X. To fuel the flame of demoralization and insubordination, autonomy and mastery—the other will-drivers that are imperative to motivation—are also stripped from schools. In an effort to foster that laser-like focus, scripted curricula (commonly referred to as "teacher-proof curricula") are adopted to ensure that educators are teaching to the standards and have solid lesson plans guiding their instruction.

Even principals are being dictated the professional development that they will provide at their schools and the initiatives that will be rolled out. While teaching was once one of the most autonomous professions (and arguably to a fault as there was little accountability and often an incoherent curriculum), with the loss of autonomy in public education we have experienced loss of morale as well, which has an equally devastating effect on our students.

Similarly, before the dawn of standardized tests and the rhetoric of America's failing schools infiltrated the shared psyche of our country's educators, teachers generally felt pretty good about their accomplishments and their impact on students (Goodson 2007). Of course we should have high standards for students, teachers, and schools. There is a clear correlation between high expectations and achievement, and it simply makes sense to set lofty goals to both communicate a belief in our students and to help them realize their full potential.

However, when schools constantly fail to measure up to these standards and teachers become the scapegoats for this failure, mastery (one of the three important motivators) could not feel further out of reach. A recent and painfully revealing study of groups of educators from different generations of teaching illustrates the effect of the current carrot-and-stick culture in public education on teacher morale.

After asking three cohorts of teachers from different eras of public education about their passions (one cohort that taught in the 1950s and 1960s, one that taught in the 1970s and 1980s, and one that taught from the 1990s to the present), only the first two groups of teachers cited teaching as a passion. The third group—the one that served as public educators from the 1990s to the present—cited mostly passions outside of their work and outside the field of education in general (Goodson 2007).

McClain and Schubert (2008) explain why this might be the case. They agree that people go into teaching with the desire to make a difference—to do something meaningful. Usually they go into the profession because they have a passion to help children become the best human beings they can become. However, as they assert,

> What happens to many teachers once they are in the classroom is too often a very different story.... They are asked to carry out teaching as a narrow range of technical activities rather than a thoughtful examination of purpose and curriculum possibility. In those schools where they must carry out "teacher-proof curricula" and unfunded mandates, many become browbeaten, angry, and embittered.... Teachers find that they become implementers of someone else's

purpose, greatly diminishing the meaning, challenges, and sense of purpose at the very heart of the teaching profession (p. 163).

However, although a great need for purpose exists, there is a virtual absence of any attention to school mission as part of public education reform in America. This is the case even though the mission is where we are able to articulate our values as stakeholders and answer fundamental questions about how to best carry out educating our students. Even the Constitution of the United States is silent on the aims of public education.

In fact, although the future of the country has always been laid at the feet of public education and in many ways we have recently moved from local control to national control of schools, the Constitution is silent on the topic of education altogether.

In arguably one of the most important industries in America—public education—where it is crucial to have passionate and masterful personnel motivated about working toward a common vision, we often end up with demoralized and hopeless individuals trudging forward through the dark, fingers crossed that they are headed in the right direction. The need to craft a shared and noble purpose for our schools has never been greater.

If it is true that what gets measured gets our focus, then we need to ensure we are measuring what is deemed most important in our children's education. If it is true that American education is failing our students and that our country's future hinges upon improving our schools, then we need to identify exactly what it is that will lead to a better future for all. Moreover, if it is true that it is a sense of purpose that inspires stakeholders to employ ingenuity, problem solving, grit, and focus in order to accomplish what seems like insurmountable goals, then we need to put that purpose at the center of all we do in our schools.

There is hope. Educators, administrators, policymakers, and students can indeed find passion and inspiration in our schools again. Identifying an overarching purpose will have a positive impact on all who are invested in public education because school mission not only plays an imperative role in motivation, but it plays a significant role in school achievement as well.

It is in the best interest of all stakeholders—whether they have data or Dewey as the driving force of their professional endeavors—to adopt a shared vision for our schools. The mission of the school has a trickle-down effect by impacting the management and organization of the building and personnel, thus affecting teaching and learning, and subsequently impacting student achievement results. If we did not always jump to the reforms and initiatives before defining the mission, we might have the very good chance of creating real change in the public education system in America.

We would very likely see a substantial rise of passion in education (from both the teachers and the learners) as well as a substantial rise in results.

As Biesta (2009) reminds us, "There is much discussion about educational processes and their improvement but very little about what such processes are supposed to bring about, so instead of simply making a case for effective education, we always need to ask 'Effective for what?'—and given that what might be effective for one particular situation or one group of students but not necessarily in another situation or for other groups of students, we also always need to ask, 'Effective for whom?'" (p. 36)

Arguably, we must be effective for our students. There is no question about that. Yet, instead, McCullough (2007) asserts,

> What one observes throughout the country is that, without a defined purpose of education, the childhood schoolhouse becomes a mere holding cell for the adulthood detention house. For those lucky enough to avoid this fate, the alternative may consist of an even greater penance—arriving at adulthood unprepared to contribute the full capacity of one's innate abilities (p. 47).

However, in order to be effective for our students, we need to make sure that the system is effective in maximizing teachers' potential as well. Recent research shows that it is the classroom teacher, more than any other variable (including students' socioeconomic status), which has the greatest impact on student learning (Hattie 2013; Marzano 2001; Reeves 2003).

Imagine what we could accomplish if American teachers were as moved by a shared vision as those who, in 1963, were on the steps of the Lincoln Memorial listening to Martin Luther King Jr. give his "I have a dream" speech. Imagine the effect that passion and drive could have on students. Imagine the consequent motivation of our students if they also understand that honorable purpose and knew in their guts that fulfilling that purpose was going to create meaningful change in society—that their schooling mattered and that they knew *why* it mattered.

Because we all yearn for that light at the end of the tunnel that moves us at our very core, it is time to have the conversation about what we want most from our schools. It is time to get on the same page about where we are headed and who benefits from heading in that direction. In order to identify a purpose that we all share and that inspires each of us to give all that we have to this most noble of all pursuits—public education—then we need to take the time to listen to each group of stakeholders invested in public education in America.

We must understand the desires of students, parents, teachers, and administrators. We must understand the hopes of politicians, business leaders, and other concerned citizens. We must also step back and form a clear picture of American society, what we value most, and the discrepancy between that ideal and our current state. And finally, we must examine the origins of public education, how the aims of our schools have changed over time, and what inspired the goals of current education reform in America. Are some pursuits of public education nobler than others?

What do we really want most for our society and our students? More importantly, what do our students and our communities most urgently need? Let us start there. Hopefully, through this exploration we can more clearly see that light at the end of the tunnel, know which direction to start moving, and be motivated to reach it.

Chapter 2

Our Past Priorities

The enormous multiplicity of expectations heaped on schools has been accumulating over the course of American history. These expectations began forming at the same time when our democratic ideals of equality, freedom, and opportunity began taking shape. Since the dawn of public schooling, the idea of social reconstructionism—or using schools to create a desired national culture—has persisted and many of the ideals on which America was founded guide the way schools operate to this day (Spring 2008; Webb 2006).

After all, public schools exist to serve the public's goals. Yet, we should not assume that the public's goals always reflect what is best for all Americans. As history shows, often public schools' primary purpose is not necessarily to improve the human condition, but rather to advance the political, social, or economic agendas of the most powerful stakeholders (Spring 2008). While we have claimed that our democratic ideals are the backbone of our society, the way those values translate into our priorities for our schools has drastically changed over time.

THE COLONIAL PERIOD

American schools originated out of the need for trained political leaders as well as the desire to create a culture on which a developing country could thrive. Colonial schools were a great example of how these ideals manifested differently in our schools across the nation. In the New England colonies, elementary education was often publicly funded and not just an opportunity for the sons of the wealthy.

The mid-Atlantic and southern colonies, however, were not quite as progressive in their educational approach. In many instances a child's social class, gender, race, or size of the town in which he lived often determined the education he received. Moreover, while freedom and independence would soon become prevalent themes in America, they did not seem to be at the forefront of education at that time.

Most colonial schools were very authoritarian in nature and structure; and the "3 R's" curriculum of reading, writing, and religion did not appear to leave much room for critical thinking or questioning of the status quo. Those students in colonial America who were gifted enough (or whose parents had enough money rather) to go on to secondary schooling had the opportunity to hold prominent roles in business or the church. However, this was not an option for most children at the time.

Moral and spiritual instructions were at the forefront of colonial education, and different colonies seemed to have different rationale for providing highly religious instruction. For some colonies and schools the purpose was individual salvation. Yet, religious instruction also seemed to be a means to foster obedience and submission. In secondary schools in New England, the purpose was to create a literate ministry.

Whatever the motive of the particular colony or town, it was clear that the role of education was quite different from its role today. Academics were less important than moral instruction. Students learned just enough academics to be able to read and recite the scripture. Academic instruction was secondary to religious instruction, especially in the New England colonies.

In addition, schools at that time focused mainly on memorization of the scripture. The goal was to produce adults who were "minimally literate" and would act according to what the schools taught. The southern colonies, in particular, believed that learning brought disobedience and, with obedience as a main theme of Christianity at that time, this posed a problem.

Yet, because the colonists had many different beliefs, the mid-Atlantic colonies did approach religious instruction with caution and different schools were established to accommodate the different denominational beliefs. This could be viewed as one of the first steps toward respecting spiritual diversity, although it had many repercussions as well. Religions and other demographics were segregated with different students getting different qualities of education and some children getting no education at all.

Finally, there was a high expectation placed upon parents during the colonial period in America to provide a solid foundation of religion and responsibility. In some colonies what parents taught their children was actually legislated. This fact suggests how important parents' roles were in educating their children spiritually and intellectually. Ultimately, the purpose of colonial education in America had little to do with economic goals of the country at the time. Rather, the social and political goals of compliance and morality guided schools' curriculum and instruction.

AMERICAN EDUCATION IN THE NINETEENTH CENTURY

During the early nineteenth century, the nation was becoming more and more industrialized. Immigrants were arriving from other countries, religious intolerance was on the rise, and education was viewed by many as the means of strengthening the nation and maintaining social order. Political agendas began to have more impact on American schools' purpose.

Horace Mann, secretary of the Massachusetts Board of Education believed that the role of schools was to "instill a common political creed in all students" (Spring 2008, p. 14). This was the beginning of the common school movement in America. The aim of common schools was to provide an equitable education for American citizens. Mann thought that if all religions and social classes had the same education, societal conflict and strife would end as a result of schooling.

Citizens would share the same political and social ideals, which would in turn "ensure the survival of the US government" (Spring 2008, p. 14). Common schools responded to the economic, religious, and social realities of that time by instituting standardized curricula, raising the bar for the teaching profession and continuing to make education more equitable for all. During this time in American history, politicians and school leaders also began to think of schools as engines for economic growth.

As the nation became increasingly industrialized, one major goal of common schools was to create a skilled workforce that would contribute to America's growing economy. Mann asserted that an educated citizenry would improve business and industry and, therefore, it was in everyone's best interest to support public education through taxation. During this time there was an effort to provide a quality education at an inexpensive cost. For the first time, the poor had the prospect for upward mobility through greater equal opportunity provided by education.

In order to avoid the pitfalls of elitism with the rich having more opportunity than the poor, Thomas Jefferson suggested that American education should be a meritocracy, or a system that provides equal opportunity for all. This system better reflected the ideals on which our country was founded and remains the claim of public schooling in America to this day.

This ideology, however, rests on the assumption that there will be no favoritism or advantage for certain demographics of students. However, at this time in history (and arguably still to this day), this idea lived only in theory but held little weight in educational practice and reality. Children in rural and urban areas often did not get an equitable education as these schools operated much differently from each other—with rural schools' calendars and enrollment reflecting the labor needs of rural regions. In this way, the industries of different areas dictated the quality of education that the children received.

In addition, many felt that immigration threatened the values and beliefs that defined America. As such, one of the goals of the common school curriculum was the "Americanization" of all children. Essentially, the desired effect of common schools was conformity. Education catered to the dominant social group by providing instruction in English only, promoting nationalism and social order in the curriculum, and teaching morality through religious (specifically Protestant) doctrine.

Likewise, the curriculum was largely based on a fictitious society with textbooks avoiding controversial issues of the time so that students would learn through a lens manufactured by stakeholders who were invested in sheltering children from prevailing social and political realities. This response likely worked in creating social order, but it most likely did not work in developing critical thinkers who would contribute to a democratic society.

Using religious instruction as the vehicle for teaching morality was also not a workable solution in that many tax-paying citizens (specifically Catholics) felt that their views were not being represented in schools. These issues eventually led to the separation of church and state. This was the common schools' response to the democratic ideal of freedom of religion as well as public funding translating to the public having a say. This absence of religion was a commonality in these schools and remains at the heart of our public school system today.

Finally, in an effort to have some control over the level of education American children received, by the late 1800s there was an increased focus on the quality of the teacher. Educational journals, "normal schools," and superintendents entered the scene. These efforts to make the quality of the education common in these schools were perceived as effective, and thus, we still have similar structures in place today.

In addition, belief systems were beginning to change, and the idea that people were fundamentally good began to inspire new teaching methods and curricula. Education became more child centered and developmentally appropriate, and people like Swiss educator, Johann Pestalozzi, established the novel philosophy of treating children with love (Webb 2006). During this time in history, the social desire for equality, freedom, and upward mobility were the driving forces for school reform.

During the late nineteenth century, patriotic exercises and fostering school spirit emerged in public schools and the Pledge of Allegiance, written by Francis Bellamy, was introduced. While equal opportunity was a prominent theme in American society and schools at that time, it was not exemplified in either. For instance, originally Bellamy had included the word "equity" in the pledge but school leaders removed it out of fear that it could imply that women and African Americans should have the same opportunity as white males.

In the 1890s, sociologist Edward Ross stated that public education should be seen as a key mechanism for social control, and he went on to say that the school—even more so than the church—was the most important institution for instilling values. Schools were called upon to create home economics classes that would play a major role in improving the quality of family life in America. In addition, these classes were hoped to change the lifestyle of American women, improve the American diet, and lead to better conditions in urban neighborhoods. It can be argued that at this time in history, social agendas dominated the reform movements of public schools.

PROGRESSIVE PERIOD

After World War I, there were dramatic changes in demographics and industry in the United States. As medical advancements were made and immigration increased, the population grew. Expansion of railroads resulted in growth in both agriculture and manufacturing. As business grew in America, corporate greed grew along with it creating horrible working conditions for many people.

Worse yet, corrupt businessmen wielded great influence in politics. In response, citizens who felt that there was a need to regulate labor, combat unfair business practices, and make government more democratic began the progressive moment. This movement challenged the ideal of limited government and aimed to improve the welfare of America's citizens. As usual, a major player in instigating this societal change was the American schools.

During this time in American history, schools became sorting machines for the labor market with students' abilities, interests, and levels of education determining their career trajectories. This reform was called tracking, in which schools essentially took on the roles of determining students' paths in life by placing them in courses that reflected their assumed skill sets.

One response of the progressive movement was to make schools more efficient, both operationally and instructionally. During this time, enrollment increased with the population such that more (and bigger) schools were built, and the facilities themselves improved. School boards became smaller and school board officials were hired using a more democratic system.

In addition, teachers were allowed a greater voice in the educational arena and educational "waste" was eliminated. School administrators attempted to ensure that every second of the school day was used as intentionally and as efficiently as possible, and it was deemed that changes in the educational system would be based on scientific inquiry.

The curriculum, however, became more child centered and was based on students' vocational or educational goals. Founded on the theories of Dewey,

Parker, Young, and Kilpatrick, instruction was focused on the social, emotional, cognitive, and physical needs and interests of the child. The progressive curriculum emphasized learning by doing, project-based discovery, and self-expression. In addition, the progressive curriculum aimed to prepare students to contribute to a democratic society.

Thus, immigrants were provided with language and citizenship training, and all pupils received a curriculum centered on American history, Christian traditions and culture, and English-only instruction. In addition, extracurricular activities such as sports teams, cheerleaders, and student government began to emerge. These were intended to build spirit and consequently prepare students for patriotism as well.

In keeping with the scientific approach to education during the progressive era, the child study movement and the measurement movement were introduced. The child study movement included the observation of children at school and at play to better understand a child's development, and, in turn, instruction was differentiated to meet the needs of that child.

Another way by which educators determined the needs of the child and made informed decisions about his schooling was through testing the student's aptitude and IQ. This increase in assessing student cognition was called the measurement movement, and, despite its criticisms, it is still a major part of American education today.

The goals of the progressive movement were to return the power to the people (as opposed to wealthy and corrupt business owners), create a workforce that could keep up with changing and growing industries, improve the general welfare of all citizens (not just the elite), and increase the duties of government in order to better regulate business and promote educational systems that would foster opportunity for all citizens.

One way to return power to the public is, of course, to educate it. The progressive movement addressed this by ensuring that schools functioned more efficiently and effectively. In hopes of creating a democratic citizenry who would contribute to the growing economy, there were increased efforts at preparing immigrants and the children of the working poor for vocations that would contribute to society. At a time when our country was focusing more and more on the rights of its citizens, it makes sense that the child-centered approach emerged in response.

Prior to the progressive era, locally controlled schools were focused on controlling students and instruction of the masses resembled human assembly lines. In the progressive era, however, the child's interests and needs dictated the curriculum and instruction. More control over schools (by stakeholders who were justly elected) and less control and oppression of the students mimicked our evolving American society where there was a push for more government influence (by way of representative democracy), and less control and oppression of American citizens.

POST-PROGRESSIVE ERA AND THE CONSERVATIVE MOVEMENT

In the 1930s, the effects of the Great Depression rippled through American industries, and education was no exception. As a result, many leaders in education summoned the federal government to provide aid to schools. In a time when the gap between rich and poor could hardly be wider, educational leaders argued that federal aid was necessary to overcome the inequities in education, and, in doing so, the inequities in society would be alleviated as well.

This increased gap between the rich and the poor also became a frustration for stakeholders of public education. In the 1940s and 1950s, a plethora of articles and books on the absence of academic rigor in American schools due to the watered down progressive movement in education started to shift the conversation about school purpose. During the mid-to-late twentieth century, two very important developments in American education were brewing.

The first important development in public education was the fight for equity in education. In the mid-twentieth century, schools were segregated by race; there were no athletic opportunities or scholarship opportunities in schools for women; many professional schools were not open to women; Mexican Americans only attended school an average of six years; and seventy-two percent of disabled children were not enrolled in public education (Streep 2002). The inequities in public education in America were profound.

Between the 1950s and 1970s parents, activists, and many students led the fight for equal opportunity in schools. The first big punch was thrown in the name of desegregation with the pivotal Supreme Court case, *Brown v. Board of Education*. At that time in American history, even in some high schools that were integrated, events and activities such as prom, student government, sports teams, and cheerleading were often segregated by race.

School districts, however, justified continued segregation under the notion of "separate but equal," which of course really meant separate but unequal. White students had better facilities, more qualified teachers, and a better education in general. In 1950, Thurgood Marshall and other attorneys from the National Association for the Advancement of Colored People (NAACP) argued the case for desegregation in the Supreme Court, and on May 17, 1954, the court announced their unanimous decision that segregation was inherently unequal.

Just because the courts said it was so, however, did not mean that the battle for equality was over. It was not until the Civil Rights Act of 1964 that racial discrimination was banned in all federally funded programs, including schools. If the Civil Rights Act was the consequence of discrimination, the Elementary and Secondary Act of 1965 was the reward for promoting equity and opportunity.

The Elementary and Secondary Act provided four billion dollars of federal aid to disadvantaged students—a level of funding that was unheard of in public education until this time in history. It wasn't until money was tied to equity that school districts finally started to seriously listen to the declaration of *Brown v. Board*. Thus, by the early 1970s, over ninety percent of southern black children attended integrated schools.

The racial inequities were not only disparities between black and white students. Mexican Americans faced tremendous adversity in the public school system as well. Students recall being told by their teachers that they would never amount to anything and being forbidden to speak in Spanish unless they wanted to be suspended or beaten with a paddle (Streep 2002).

During the early 1960s, textbooks and other school resources bared no reflection of the Mexican American culture whatsoever. The message in schools was essentially that if you wanted to amount to anything, you needed to be less of who you were . . . unless you were white. The goal of the schools continued to be the Americanization of children—especially children from Latino communities.

Because of these inequities, a movement began to build among Mexican American students and parents demanding more from their schools. They wanted to see their history honored in their textbooks, they wanted to be able to have the same access to the curriculum that English speakers had, and they wanted to be respected by their teachers.

The federal government stepped in and as an extension of President Johnson's War on Poverty, the Bilingual Education Act was enacted to meet the needs of children whose first language was not English. Moreover, in 1974, bilingual education received backing from the U.S. Supreme Court when they declared that same treatment is not synonymous with equal treatment and that children should have equal access to education by having the opportunity to learn in their first language. In the mid-1970s the federal government published teaching materials in various languages and allocated almost seventy million dollars for bilingual programs in schools.

Feminism was also gaining traction in education during the Civil Rights era. In the early 1970s, only one percent of medical and law degrees went to women. Females lacked the same opportunities their male counterparts were privy to in public schools. Girls' inability to participate in school sports initiated the class-action suit filed by the Women's Equity Action League in 1974. The passing of Title IX was the first step toward educational equality for women and girls.

However, the lack of opportunity to participate in sports was not the only obstacle that girls were up against in schools. Curricular resources were filled with gender biases of all kinds. Texts for young readers portrayed boys as active, smart, and strong, whereas they portrayed girls as passive, kind, and cute. In the higher grades, girls were offered fewer advanced placement courses and steered away from disciplines like math and science.

Equal opportunity in sports did not exist either, with some school districts spending up to 450 times more money on boys' sports than that of girls'. Over time, parents and students pressured school districts to comply with Title IX, and over time, the gender bias in classrooms and textbooks has decreased. Soon, women began earning more college and graduate degrees than men, and the number of girls in sports grew from one percent in the early 1970s to forty percent by the 1990s.

In 1976, students with disabilities were the last group to receive a national platform for equity in education through civil rights legislation. This legislation required schools to provide resources and training that would give students with disabilities equal access to the curriculum.

In addition, schools were required to include students with disabilities in mainstream classrooms rather than separating them into different rooms or different schools. In the Civil Rights era, public schools not only reflected the tensions and changes of American society to become more equitable for disadvantaged students, but that focus on equity also propelled society forward by creating a society that valued diversity more than ever before.

The second major development in the mid-to-late twentieth century was curriculum reform in the aftermath of Sputnik and the swinging of the pendulum away from progressivism in education. The launch of Sputnik brought with it the heightened philosophy of education as the tool for competing in a global economy. As Americans believed that their status as a world superpower was being threatened, progressive education was trumped by the need for a more rigorous academic curriculum.

The fear that Sputnik evoked in the federal government was possibly greater than the fear inspired by the Great Depression. Not only did this increase the federal government's involvement in education, but it influenced the direction in which the federal government took education as well. No longer was government support just about promoting equity or helping public schools get on their feet; now support was directly aimed at the areas of math and science, and there was a real sense of urgency to create programs and curricula designed to help the Americans surpass the Soviets.

This marked the dawn of the conservative movement in education in America. While the word "conservative" might normally make one think of tradition and preservation of the status quo, those descriptors do not fit the educational conservatism at the end of the twentieth century. However, conservatives might also be thought of as being somewhat risk-averse, which does seem to describe the policymakers of this era.

For a long time in America, progressivism was the predominant mind-set in education. Progressivism, though, was also a risk.

The progressives were hopeful that a child-centered education would create ethical and inspired citizens who were true to themselves and were also constructive members of society. However, the hope of the progressives slowly gave way to the fear of the conservatives when this type of education did not seem to bring about quantifiable results. Therefore, although the aim of conservatism in this era was not to uphold the status quo but rather to create a new vision for the future, it seems policymakers thought it was less risky to revamp the system all together than to continue on the same path.

Conservatism has been increasing in influence within American education ever since. For the past two decades in American history, standards—which were aimed at bringing rigor back into the schools—have been the engine behind virtually every major reform in America. In 1983, policymakers warned U.S. citizens through the powerful treatise *A Nation at Risk* that there was an epidemic of mediocrity, which had infiltrated our country's education system.

The authors of *A Nation at Risk* were fearful that Americans would soon be surpassed as the world's scientific and technological superpower. This argument inspired fear in schools' stakeholders, and by the early 1990s, the federal government's role in education had increased dramatically.

In 1996, at the National Education Summit, bipartisan leaders formed the organization, Achieve. The goal was to lead standards-based education reform efforts across America. Soon all states had adopted standards for student learning and systems of accountability that measured students' progress. Over time, however, problems began to arise as educators and policymakers realized that some states had set their standards too low and that there was too much variance among the standards that each state adopted.

At the beginning of the twenty-first century, President George W. Bush attempted to address these issues by introducing unprecedented reform in education titled No Child Left Behind (NCLB). This reform brought with it even more presence of the federal government in public education (in both policy and funding) and set the stage for what would eventually be a national assessment of America's students. NCLB provided the framework for increased standardization and accountability in U.S. schools, and its goal was to have all students meeting grade level standards by 2014.

The provisions under NCLB required teachers to be "highly qualified" and mandated that schools across the country make sufficient "Annual Yearly Progress" toward meeting the goals of the reform. Moreover, the federal government put in place rewards for high performance and sanctions for inadequate performance. Many argue that NCLB has fundamentally changed the role of the federal government in education from providing support and services to increasing students' academic achievement.

The democratic administration that followed, under the leadership of President Barack Obama, solidified and expanded upon their new role in public education through Race to the Top, a reform policy with a new name but similar goals. Consequently, in 2009, as part of a partnership with the National Governors Association (NGA) and the Council of Chief State School Officers (CCSSO), and in collaboration with teachers, school administrators, and national experts in curriculum and instruction, Achieve developed the Common Core State Standards.

These standards were specifically created with the goal of ensuring college and career readiness for all American students and were hoped to alleviate the problem of varying standards between the states. After much feedback and revision, the standards were officially launched in June 2010. Since the launch of the Common Core State Standards, most states in the union have adopted these national standards, and accountability based reform has remained on the rise.

As the conservative movement continues to create monumental change in education purpose and reform, many citizens wonder if and when the pendulum of American education will once again reach its peak and begin swinging back the other way.

THE PENDULUM SWINGS OF AMERICAN EDUCATIONAL PHILOSOPHY

Over the course of American history, the goals of public schools have always been directly influenced by the political, social, and economic goals of those who have held the power in America. As the goals of American leaders change, school reform is quick to follow, and more and more expectations are placed on schools. Meanwhile, the pendulum of reform swings back and forth from more child-centered purposes to more society-centered purposes without anyone stopping to wonder if what is best for the child might also be best for society.

The only constant in American education has been change. And, changes in education, whether progressive or conservative, have always been somewhat reactive instead of proactive—meaning that policymakers consistently have used education as a major means of "fixing" society's ills as opposed to looking forward and determining what kind of society we want to live in and using that ideal to determine the purpose of American schools.

Some scholars argue that the dawn of the twenty-first century brought us closer to our initial dream of the American common school by creating a rigorous set of standards that all students are expected to master and by trying to hold schools accountable for making sure that students do master those standards. Over the course of American history we have tried to improve teacher effectiveness, we have attempted to find ways for the disadvantaged to have equal access to a quality education, we have tried teaching the fundamentals to all, and we have tried individualizing the learning for each child.

While we were getting closer to the core of many of these complex issues, I doubt anyone can claim that they have been solved. By the early twenty-first century there is still inequity in the American education system. Minorities and students of poverty still do not have the same opportunities and quality of education compared to others. While there are increased expectations and rigor in schools, high stakes tests cannot measure those life skills and lessons that are often most important in personal and societal growth. Many claim that they really cannot even measure the critical thinking skills that the conservative movement in education hoped to bring about.

Have any of these past and present reforms really solved the major issues in education or society? Have any of the long-term goals we have set for schools been realized? It is hard to tell. Social, economic, and political problems in America have definitely been addressed through public education, and many situations in these areas have improved over time, but issues in society and education are so complex that solving societal problems is not a straightforward endeavor.

As we embark on solutions to society's problems, we uncover multiple other issues that also need to be addressed, and we create new and different problems as an unintended result of these solutions. One might argue, however, that we have been successful in shining a light on many issues in education such as equity for minorities, students with disabilities, and students in poverty; the need for high expectations and a way to assess whether or not students are meeting those expectations; and teacher development and accountability.

With every new study that comes out about the importance of equity in education, the power of effective teaching, the role of diversity in creating empathy, etc., we work toward the improvement of society and the human condition. Just as importantly, we also uncover more that we need to address through public education. In the areas that American society has improved, perhaps we can assume that education had a part in those positive changes.

To be fair, where society has changed for the worse we might assume that education had a role in that as well. It seems that while we are always striving for equal rights and opportunity for American citizens we have become more and more tolerant and accepting of diversity in our nation. Maybe past reforms in education have contributed to this growth as a country. In addition, we are still one of the most technologically advanced and creative nations in the world. Perhaps the swinging pendulum has somehow managed to balance rigorous standards with child-centered teaching.

Common sense tells us that every educational theory and practice has benefits and repercussions. One side of the educational pendulum impacts society both positively and negatively, just as the opposite side does. For instance, progressivism and its focus on the child as the center of the teaching and learning created students who were confident, creative, and inspired to continue learning throughout life.

However, they were lagging in some basic skills, and the decreased rigor and focus in many subject areas made it difficult to create an American citizenry who would propel our country forward in the global marketplace. Traditionalists and their reforms brought rigor and focus back into schools, although often at the expense of the child or at the expense of equity and opportunity for minorities and the disadvantaged.

It seems we have never *purposefully* implemented a reform that balances both ends of the pendulum well. Rather, we swing to one side, get scared of the consequences of being so far over, react, and swing to the other side. Since this cycle began in American education, it has not stopped. Priorities in education reflect priorities in society, and vice versa.

It is imperative that we continue to examine and identify what is most important to us as Americans and foster that in our schools. We must never lose sight of our values. Indeed, it is those values that determine the purpose for our schools, and as society drives education forward, education in turn propels society forward.

Chapter 3

Our Current Priorities

COLLEGE AND CAREER READY

Since the early 1980s, stakeholders in education have been worried about the state of America's schools, and many—from secretaries of education to Bill Gates—have blamed public education for raising a generation of Americans who do not have the scientific and technological skills or knowledge required to be a major player in the global economy. While *A Nation at Risk* presented similar solutions as those that were presented in more recent education reform, until recently, those solutions had not been realized. This began a long-standing debate about whether or not states should adopt a common set of national standards.

However, a growing body of research over the past decade has begun to point to the increased importance of postsecondary education. Advancements in technology began to deplete jobs in America that required routine skills while more and more jobs that required sophisticated problem-solving and communication skills emerged. In addition, according to Carnevale, Smith, and Strohl (2009), sixty-two percent of U.S. jobs in 2018 will require some sort of postsecondary education. (By contrast, in 1973 only twenty-eight percent of jobs required education beyond high school.)

This shortage of workers with degrees in higher education has driven up wages for those who have postsecondary degrees with workers with bachelor's degrees earning seventy-four percent more than workers with high school diplomas. If this trend continues, by 2025, workers with a college education will be earning twice as much as those with only a high school education. However, at the onset of the Common Core movement, the supply of college-educated workers was not rising fast enough to meet the demand

and many state-adopted standards did not reflect this growing need for critical thinking and increased scientific and technological skills.

For instance, community members and educators had originally created each state's standards with varied or ambiguous criteria (not necessarily aimed at preparing students for an ever-changing workforce). To meet the set criteria and to please local politicians, many of these state's standards began to resemble a giant laundry list of learning that emphasized breadth of skill over depth of understanding.

The process of creating the Common Core, however, was different. From the outset, leaders established what they claimed was clear criteria for what they wanted students to leave school knowing and being able to do. The Common Core project used a backward design planning model by developing anchor standards for English language arts and mathematics that students would need to master by the end of high school. Then working backward, they created standards at each grade that would build on each other and lead students to those anchor standards.

In addition, standards were developed under the umbrella of college and career readiness, and topics and skills that were not essential to either criterion were not included. Writers of the Common Core consulted business owners and collected evidence from colleges as well as members of the workforce prior to the creation of the standards. They bought university textbooks and studied the kinds of reading and mathematics that students would be expected to have under their belts as freshmen.

They then asked businessmen and members of the higher education community to verify the inferences they made about what students should know and be able to do by the time they completed twelfth grade. This work became the foundation upon which the standards were written. The stated goal of the national standards was to specify the essential skills and knowledge in a format that made it clear to teachers what they needed to teach as well as clarify for educational leaders and policymakers what they needed to assess.

The goals essentially would outline the *what* and the *how* of teaching and learning. The hopes were that the Common Core movement would lead to more consistent academic expectations of American students as well as more accurate research and data reflecting what works in education. Although the *why* received less focus and attention than the standards and plan for implementation, it was declared to be "college and career readiness."

For decades, leaders in politics and education have been proposing that standards are the foundation upon which nearly all else rests. Standards it seems, while intended to articulate the *what* and not the *why*, have become the current end goal in public education, rather than the means to an end. Standards inform lesson planning, teacher preparation, professional development, assessments, and systems of accountability.

Proponents of the Common Core movement argue that if the standards are rigorous, clear, and are guided by purposeful intentions, then they have the potential to lead our schools down promising paths. In other words, who needs a transparent and clearly articulated purpose when our plan is strong enough?

In 2009, President Obama, alongside Secretary of Education, Arne Duncan, introduced Race to the Top, a 4.3 billion dollar plan to improve American public schools—with strings attached. Obama's program outlined key reforms that states would have to embrace in order to qualify for Race to the Top funding. Part of that "key reform" was the adoption of the Common Core Standards and their accompanying assessments.

By 2011, forty-seven states and the District of Columbia had committed to replacing their state standards with the Common Core, and forty-five of those states had joined one of the two assessment consortia that were working on replacing existing tests with rigorous assessments based on the new standards. While language arts and mathematics are the focus of the Common Core, the Core expects that literacy standards be taught in history, social studies, science, and technical subjects.

The hope is that students will learn literacy skills that are specific to these disciplines in addition to the literacy they learn in language arts classes. The idea is that this exponentially increases the amount of time students spend practicing literacy skills and that the skills students learn simulate the skills they will need in college and the workforce. In language arts there are key cognitive strategies that students are expected to develop at each grade level.

They include analyzing how and why individuals, events, and ideas develop and interact over the course of a text; integrating and evaluating content presented in diverse formats and media; reading and comprehending complex literary and informational texts independently and proficiently; developing and strengthening writing as needed by planning, revising, editing, rewriting, or trying new approaches; using technology to produce and publish writing and interact with others; and conducting research projects demonstrating understanding of the subject under investigation.

The standards also identify specific mathematical practices that students at all levels should master, including making sense of problems and persevering in solving them; reasoning abstractly and quantitatively; constructing viable arguments and critiquing the reasoning of others; modeling with mathematics; using appropriate tools strategically; attending to precision; looking for and making use of structure; and looking for expressing regularity in repeated reasoning.

Initial reviews of the standards indicate that they do, in fact, reflect the expectations of colleges and universities around the country. One survey done by the Education Policy Improvement Center (EPIC) at the University of Oregon determined that both teachers and students agreed that the standards directly reflected the knowledge and skills that students should master in preparation for postsecondary education.

They found that the emphasis in the Common Core on reading complex texts was aligned to the expectations and texts that students were expected to read at the college level. In addition, the increased emphasis on technical, informational, and persuasive writing over narrative writing in the Common Core also reflected the types of writing that college students were expected to utilize. The same congruency was true for mathematics.

Proponents of the Common Core speculate that implementation of the new standards would be a much-needed departure from rote memorization and drill-and-practice activities, learning through worksheets, and elaborate teaching to the test practices. The hope is that the new national standards support content acquisition through an engaging and challenging curriculum by drawing on a variety of research-based instructional strategies (Conley 2011).

In addition, the Common Core Standards are expected to have leverage that reaches to college and career readiness and beyond. One final promise of the Common Core is that it promotes the skills and knowledge necessary to foster a democratic citizenry including critical thinking, evaluation of text, persuasive writing, speaking, and listening.

The Common Core State Standards are a set of shared goals developed around what leaders believe will help students succeed. They are not a curriculum. Therefore, decisions about how best to teach these standards are being made at the local level, but the fact remains: the goal is that all students in America will be held to the same academic expectations. This undoubtedly raises the question of whether education will become more equitable for America's children and whether the American system of education is closer than ever in realizing its dream of the common school.

There are other questions that are being raised as well. Whether the Common Core Standards move our students to college and career readiness might not be the most pressing question on the table. The most pressing question might be, is college and career readiness the most urgent need of our students and our society? Should it be schools' greatest purpose?

If college and career readiness is schools' greatest purpose, should we be addressing students' *desire* to go to college or *passion* for a particular career or field of study? If college and career readiness is not schools' greatest purpose, how do we define student success? Is it a degree? Is it a lucrative career? Should traditional definitions of success even be the primary goal of public education? What does the Common Core indicate about the current social, political, and economic ideals of America's leaders?

Opponents of the Common Core say that standardization is not the driving force behind an effective education system, but rather it is creativity that leads to success. Some state that while Americans have been hearing for decades about the threat of losing our status as a scientific and economic superpower, the fact is that the United States continues to dominate the world as the most technologically and scientifically advanced nation.

For example, the United States created the core innovations behind the global digital revolution, the United States houses the leaders of the Internet and computer industries, and it is still a world leader in patents, with the majority of patents being issued to American citizens (Zhao 2006). Moreover, the countries that spurred the initial concern behind *A Nation at Risk* (including Japan and South Korea) have since faced economic recessions of their own.

Zhao (2006) argues that reformers could be wrong about what the real problems in U.S. education are as well as what it takes to compete in a global economy. Zhao asserts that it is the spirit behind the American people, not their knowledge and skills, that has helped the United States remain a global superpower. He states that the success of our country lies in an education system that fosters creativity and risk taking—attributes that cannot be measured by standardized testing.

He also points to the irony that while American education is changing to look more like that of China or Japan, these same systems are reforming education in their countries to look more like the United States by attempting to foster more innovation and creativity in their students. When the standards were developed, not only did the writers consult colleges and businesses about what students should know and be able to do to be prepared for higher education and the workforce, but they also went to great lengths to match the academic expectations set for students in higher-performing countries like Singapore and South Korea.

The hope was that higher standards would help close the achievement gap between lower income and minority students and students from more affluent families. The writers reasoned that raising the standards would drive publishers and test makers to create better curricula that lead to excellence by ensuring that teachers, principals, and parents would know exactly what it takes to be successful in the future.

However, the writers of the Common Core did not anticipate the bipartisan opposition that would soon follow. In 2013, anti-Common Core momentum began to grow when a father in North Carolina (who also happened to be an engineer) posted a "Common Core" math question from his son's homework along with a letter he had written to his son's teacher in response saying that even he could not make sense of the problem.

Soon Glen Beck and other conservative pundits used this post to propel the discussion in opposition to the Common Core forward. Comedians jumped on board as well, and soon the American public heard Common Core math jokes on late night TV. Some opponents, however, stated that the standards weren't rigorous enough. They argued that the Common Core Standards were not necessarily improvements from the previous states' standards.

For instance, the Thomas B. Fordham Institute determined that some states' standards were already equivalent in rigor to the Common Core English language arts and mathematics standards. Indeed, California, Indiana, and the District of Columbia imposed standards that were clearly better than the Common Core in the area of English language arts. If these standards were better than the Common Core, then one could infer that students in these states would be demonstrating the academic success that the Common Core Standards promise to create.

However, this was not the case. If states with similarly rigorous standards did not reach the level of academic achievement that was expected with the Common Core, how can we assume that the Common Core will transform student achievement in America? And, should we assume that by simply transforming student achievement we will inherently transform students' future success and the success of the country in turn?

In addition, critics of the Common Core wonder what will prevent the Common Core from becoming one more initiative that dies before full implementation. What will ensure the depth of implementation across the country that is necessary to test the effectiveness of the Common Core initiative? Even more concerning to some is the idea that knowing *what* to teach does not necessarily guarantee that teachers will know *how* to teach it.

A teacher may know that a fifth grader needs to master the skills and concepts behind surface area in mathematics, but if that fifth grader comes in lacking in many prerequisite skills, simply knowing that a fifth grader must demonstrate mastery of surface area per the Common Core State Standards will not likely help the teacher or student in meeting that goal. Some assert that knowing *how* best to instruct students is equally important as knowing *what* they must learn. Would any child ever be "left behind" if all educators needed to know was *what* that child must learn?

There are many Democrats and Republicans who support the Common Core, however. Those in favor of the Common Core argue that today's students are reading and doing math two or three grade levels above where they were in the 1990s. They state that with NCLB all the focus was on getting the lowest students to move up, which actually happened in most cases; however, it was often at the expense of the higher students.

Often their learning was minimal or stagnant because so much attention was being paid to the number of students who passed the test as opposed to the growth of each student. The Common Core Standards and the accountability systems that have followed in their wake, however, raise the expectations for students and require all students to make sufficient growth. Thus, with the Common Core, proponents argue that we aren't just focusing on our lowest students; we are focusing on all students.

Moreover, many teachers support the Common Core. They argue that continuing to foster low expectations and dumb down the curriculum certainly won't lead to future success. Proponents of the Common Core remind us that there is a difference between having high standards for success and having standardized tests rule our decision-making processes in schools.

Even those who do not like the overemphasis on test results state that the standards themselves are not responsible for the bad curricular choices or hyper focus on test results. They also argue that because things are always changing in public education, it is time we follow through with a reform and are patient with waiting to see the results of its implementation.

However, whether or not the standards will lead to mastery of the specified knowledge and skills students need to gain by twelfth grade is beside the point to many. Mulligan (2014) argues that American youth today have been conditioned to see their grades (and thus the learning) as a means to an end. They believe that the reason for getting good grades is to impress college admissions officers and future employers; the reason for doing community service is to have something to put on your resume; and the reason for participating in sports, music, or art is to look well rounded or get a scholarship—not because these things invoke passion in them.

Mulligan asserts that this is why many of these students don't do well in college: they are motivated by goals that are not noble or inspiring. They leave their K–12 education without knowing who they even are, what they enjoy, or what they stand for. There is little to no intrinsic value for their learning or hard work, and thus, when they get to college where it is expected that students learn for learning's sake, they begin to fall apart at the seams.

Even though most schools' mission statements say something about creating "lifelong learners," we actually teach our children that outcomes are more important than the process of learning or the enjoyment of learning. The only thing that we show students that we value (and that they should value) is the endgame. Yet, the endgame is not intrinsically rewarding for many of them.

It is hard for students to think past an hour from now—much less past next Tuesday—and certainly hard for them to think of college and career readiness, especially for our students from poverty who are historically underserved by education and underrepresented in higher education. We would likely prepare our students better for college and career if we made the process of learning the reward by making learning enjoyable and engaging.

Warner (2014), a college professor of freshman students, states that even if our end goal is and should be college and career readiness, the Common Core's and federal government's version of readiness is not his version. He states that, in his experience, the skills and standards with which students enter college (as long as they demonstrate basic competence) are not as important for their success in college as the attitudes they bring to the learning.

Rather, Warner suggests that the most successful students—rather than being the ones who have mastered K–12 competencies—are the ones who are curious, can self-regulate, have passion, are empathetic, and have a healthy skepticism of authority.

In fact, according to much research, there shouldn't even be a debate around the importance of teaching these soft skills (e.g., self-regulation, empathy) in school.

Future employers want applicants who are well rounded and have strong social/emotional skills. Actually, more important to employers than technical skill and knowledge is adaptability, agility, creativity, collaboration, and great communication. In order to focus on these soft skills in schools we need to add some of the less tangible aspects of teaching and learning. The culture of the school is as imperative to college and career readiness as is the classroom instruction. A positive culture promotes engagement and hope and fosters both the hard and soft skills that are necessary for success.

If what we desire is for the United States to lead the globe in innovation and economic prosperity, then we need to look at what current research says about the commonalities of effective businesses and business leaders. Research has uncovered that the one thing that sets apart the successful leaders from their less successful counterparts is social intelligence.

Success in big business is less about skill, knowledge, technical ability, work ethic, and organization as it is about how you make *others* feel. One study found that workers whose employers demonstrated poor social intelligence experienced emotional exhaustion four times that of their colleagues who had socially intelligent leaders (Boyatzis & Goleman 2008).

Finally, educators and others have voiced concern over the fact that there has not been any research shown that indicates that the Common Core State Standards will have a positive impact on teaching, learning, or even test scores. The official Common Core website does state that the standards are based on research, but it does not elaborate on what or where that research is centered. This begs the question of whether or not this new reform is simply change for change's sake and is yet again another swing of the pendulum in the American education system. Only time will tell.

Beane (2013) states that there are two main positions behind almost all curriculum reform over the last century in American education. One such position is that students need to be prepared to function in society and need to be taught the skills and concepts that will help them enter the workforce and become productive and happy citizens. This stance is called social efficiency. The other position, liberal studies, asserts that the major purpose of schools is to impart skills and knowledge from traditional and cultural resources, such as classic literature.

Through understanding history, liberal studies proponents claim that students can apply its enduring understandings and are more likely to become critical thinkers and lead an intellectual life. The Common Core may be the first reform in American history to embrace and reflect both theories. For decades, the pendulum of American education has been swinging back and forth from relevance to rigor. Is this yet another swing of the pendulum, or has it found its perfect balance in the Common Core?

Ackerman (2003) proposed that the ideal curriculum would be the one that tapped into the strengths of both progressivism and traditionalism. He suggested ten commandments for education that would most benefit student learning. These commandments include (from the traditional "tablet") teaching that which is of deepest value; teaching with rigor; upholding standards of excellence; being efficient with time; honoring the knowledge of the disciplines; and (from the progressive "tablet") remembering the value each child brings to the learning; remembering that not all standards are equally important for each child; avoiding a drill and memorization focus; honoring each child's perspective and opinion; and teaching in a holistic manner.

While the Common Core Standards do not embody all of these commandments, and while there is much controversy surrounding the Core, the foundations upon which the Core was built claim to honor philosophies from both the traditional and progressive camps. The Common Core Standards are most certainly rigorous. However, one could argue that they are relevant as well.

They foster critical thinking, while emphasizing the interconnectedness of ideas and disciplines. What is more, these new national standards place more weight than ever before on student voice. From kindergarten through twelfth grade, students are expected to engage in continual thoughtful analysis of a variety of texts on which they form opinions, make claims, and take a stance through ongoing, reflective, and collaborative learning.

This not only sends the message to students that they matter, but this practice also fosters the democratic foundation on which our country is built. In this sense, the Common Core honor the individual student *and* serve the purpose for which this reform was initiated—to better our society by producing critical thinkers who propel us forward.

However, lost in these debates is the critical question of purpose. Specifically, does our tunnel vision on results as measured by standardized tests kill the aims of the Common Core in its tracks because we still have yet to articulate an inspiring purpose that we can all get behind at the practitioner level?

While it is doubtful that we have found a perfect balance in *what* and *how* we teach because of the hyper focus on results, it is even more doubtful that we have landed on an inspiring and transparent *why* we teach into which all stakeholders can invest their passion and their commitment.

Yet, this elusive purpose for our schools could be the missing link to the success of public education in America. If what we teach is so important to the success of students and the advancement of society, then it is crucial that educators and the public can articulate a common philosophy of what defines success and what our hopes are for our students and our society. Is economic superiority our aim? Is it personal fulfillment? Is it peace?

Ackerman mentioned in his commandments that we should teach that which is of deepest value. The Common Core Standards likely have value, but do they reflect our *deepest* values? Can we trust that those educational leaders, policymakers, and businessmen were not shortsighted in their aims when they sat down at the table to develop these national standards?

It is time to step back from the global rat race and realize that we are *all* stakeholders in education. What is it that we value most? What is it that is essential for our children to learn? The Common Core Standards may hold pieces to the puzzle, but my guess is that they do not paint the whole picture.

TEACHER EFFECTIVENESS

Riding the wave of the Common Core initiative is the teacher effectiveness movement. And, as with the Common Core movement, there are two sides to the debate. One camp argues that too often we use poverty as an excuse to not insist on higher standards and greater achievement from students. They suggest that the reason we have low performance and such a large achievement gap in this country is that we have so many bad teachers and that the key to closing the achievement gap is in hiring better educators and improving current instruction.

Bill Gates, prominent education reformer, philanthropist, business mogul, inventor, computer programmer, and founder of the Bill and Melinda Gates Foundation is one of the key players in the teacher effectiveness movement. He states that the more his research team investigated improving education, the more they realized that solid teaching was the most crucial aspect of student success.

This finding is congruent with the claims of other leading researchers in public education including Robert Marzano and John Hattie. Both present meta-analyses that suggest classroom instruction is the largest variable in increasing student outcome (Hattie 2013; Marzano 2001). According to Gates (2009), a top-quartile teacher increases the performance of his students—based on test scores—by over ten percent in a single year, which is a huge difference from teachers in the bottom quartile.

He asserts that if every student in America had a top-quartile teacher for two years in a row, we would rival the top performing countries in the world. And, if every student in America had a top-quartile teacher for four years in a row, we would blow every other country out of the water. An interesting finding is that effective teaching has nothing to do with years of experience or amount of schooling. However, the current pay scale for teachers is based on exactly these two criteria: seniority and masters' degrees/credits.

However, while it is easy to rule out the things that don't contribute to effective teaching, it is much harder to pinpoint what does. That does not stop us, however, from trying to replicate and reward effective teaching. The teacher effectiveness movement, though, is really about using students' test scores to evaluate educators. In the past couple of years, forty-three states have applied for and received Race to the Top grants or NCLB waivers by adopting teacher-evaluation systems.

In 2011, the Obama administration allowed states to apply for flexibility from some requirements under the Elementary and Secondary Education Act (ESEA), which is better known as NCLB, under the condition that they would need to implement new teacher-evaluation systems that used standardized test scores as a means of evaluating teachers. Other reforms that the waiver mandated states can implement are college- and career-readiness standards and teacher-accountability plans.

What's more, the pressure that the federal government is putting on states and districts to implement these systems is causing them to implement systems in a rush before fully vetting their effectiveness. Proponents of this reform, however, state that we have no time to dawdle because there is a disparity in the quality of instruction that students in poverty and students from more affluent communities receive, and this disparity only continues to widen the achievement gap in America.

Gates (2009) suggests that we can learn how to narrow this gap by studying teachers of low-income students who are getting stellar results. One example he provides is the Knowledge Is Power Program (KIPP) schools. These charter schools take the most impoverished students and send ninety-six percent of their graduates to four-year colleges. What is unique about these teachers, he says, is that they constantly collaborate around data, and they celebrate their successes constantly, whereas in regular public schools, teachers are rarely told how good they are and are rarely collecting data that indicates the effectiveness of their instruction.

Gates's findings are congruent with the findings of Karen Chenoweth, author of three books on highly effective schools and teachers. Chenoweth (2015) synthesized the factors that led to unprecedented achievement of students from poverty and minority students and found that teacher collaboration and the analysis of data were central to student success. She also found another factor that is not often cited in the research on effective schools—that all of the effective schools nurtured trust among administrators, students, parents, and teachers through strong personal relationships.

In the schools that were getting amazing results, stakeholders practiced social intelligence. The irony here is that one of the sad effects of the current culture in America has been the dehumanization and distrust of educators. In systems such as Finland's, which are often studied in order to gather insight into why they are so successful, teachers are regarded as highly as doctors and lawyers. In fact, education policies in Finland focus more on school effectiveness than teacher effectiveness (Strauss 2013).

And, even though some of the most prominent researchers in education tout the classroom teacher as having the largest impact on student success, there is other research that contradicts these conclusions. A commonly used finding is that between ten and twenty percent of the variance measured in student achievement is due to what happens in the classroom, and between ten to twenty percent of the variance measured in student achievement is attributed to school climate and leadership.

That leaves around two-thirds of what students achieve as beyond the influence of schools (Strauss 2013). Thus, school culture and the culture of the students' families and greater community have just as much influence, if not more, on student achievement as the classroom teacher. Yet, these cultural factors are hard to implement and even harder to measure, so we turn our hopes to standardized assessments as the sole means of measuring teachers' contributions to students' learning.

One of the problems with this is that we assume that current and future success—the current achievement gap and the future economic gap—can be measured by standardized assessments. Educators understand that first, much more goes into student success than simply what is measured on standardized assessments, and second, it is the entire system that contributes to that success.

In the successful school systems around the world that are scoring high in international rankings, teachers state that they feel empowered by their leaders and coworkers. In Finland, half of the teachers surveyed said they would quit teaching if their evaluation were based on students' standardized test scores (Strauss 2013).

The lack of validity in using test scores to evaluate teachers is why the Association for Supervision and Curriculum Development (ASCD), an education advocacy group, is calling for a two-year moratorium on using standardized assessment results for teacher or school evaluations. This is in the wake of a much larger national push to cut back on testing in general and limit their use as accountability measures (DeNisco 2015).

ASSESSMENT AND MEASUREMENT

Since 2002, annual reading and math assessments for students in America have been the cornerstone of federal education law. These assessments are used for many purposes, including to inform instruction, inform parents, compare student results to others in the district, state, and nation, and to evaluate teachers. Two government-funded consortia have developed computer-based assessments for the Common Core Standards that are being widely adopted by the states for use with general population students. These assessments are PARCC (the Partnership for Assessment Readiness for College and Careers) and SBAC (Smarter Balanced Assessment Consortium).

These tests differ from previous standardized assessments used by the states in a few ways. First, both tests assess the Common Core State Standards and will be administered for the first time in the spring of 2015. Also, both assessments claim to have more sophisticated testing technology so that they are able to capture students' critical thinking skills, not simply rote memorization. This is done through the use of performance-based tasks and technology-enhanced items.

Combined components will assess student growth, not just where they are at one point in time. Finally, in addition to the summative, end-of-the-year assessments, both tests offer formative and interim testing tools intended to help teachers and parents identify students' strengths and weaknesses so that they can target interventions and extensions before the year is over (Houghton Mifflin Harcourt n.d.).

Proponents of these new assessments have argued that the tests are better on many counts. The fact that they are able to assess more real-world problem-solving skills and communication is just one example of how these tests are superior to the various standardized assessments that states used previously. This, however, has not stopped the backlash from the general public about their implementation.

Some claim that the tests themselves are great, but the obsession and emphasis around the testing and testing results are producing unintended and negative consequences for children. Others claim that not only are we too focused on testing, but the tests themselves are inappropriate and poorly written for students. Even one public school district superintendent has spoken out about his concerns regarding the PARCC standardized assessment, claiming that because of the sheer amount of time it takes to administer this assessment significant learning time is lost. In addition, he says that the test itself is not useful beyond providing legislators with a data point.

It is not useful to students, parents, or teachers as the results do not come out until after the student has left his or her class and moved on to the next year of school. Because of this, the test cannot be used to inform instruction.

Another concern is that the technology required by the assessment is beyond what many districts have access to or are able to prepare students. The technology alone can skew the results of any assessment, and if students miss the problems it may be solely due to the fact that they are not familiar with the technology (Strauss 2015).

Proponents, however, argue that if we continue to let these concerns stand in our way, we will never stick with an initiative or reform long enough to assess its effects with students. There will be a learning curve with any new reform, but simply abandoning it out of discomfort with that curve will not do students any favors.

Proponents state that rather it is the schools' and districts' responsibilities to reduce testing anxiety, prepare students better by investing in current technologies, and continue to think outside the box and scaffold the instruction to make learning accessible for students rather than simply abandoning our high expectations because of the false notion that students cannot meet them.

Opponents' voices, however, are getting louder and louder. In many communities parents are forming opt-out groups and requesting that their children be exempt from taking the test. In addition, the Council of Chief State School Officers and some of the largest school districts in America have been vocal about decreasing the number of standardized assessments that students take. In fact, national teachers unions and other traditionally democratic groups are behind the movement of decreasing standardized assessments in schools.

Even Education Secretary, Arne Duncan, admits that he has concerns about testing, although he backs them as an important educational tool. Because of all this pushback, though, Republican Senate aides are drafting a bill that would eliminate the federal mandate on standardized testing. So, what do opponents propose as alternatives to these standardized assessments? After all, we still have to know how students are doing and the effects our instruction is producing.

One idea is sampling. Those in favor of sampling suggest that students should be given the same assessments, just fewer of them. Similar to the NAEP (National Assessment of Educational Progress) text and the PISA (Program for International Student Assessment) assessment, where a random sampling is taken of students across the nation or globe in order to get an idea of how students are doing compared to other states or countries, proponents of sampling state that we should use the Smarter Balanced and PARCC assessments in the same way since these assessments are intended to provide summative rather than formative information anyway (Kamenetz 2015).

Other ideas are to implement stealth assessments and/or multiple measures instead. Stealth assessments are assessments embedded in the curriculum so that students are not even aware that their responses and work are being recorded and filed. Because so much of the curriculum is now delivered and practiced through different modes of technology, it is easier than ever to collect digital portfolios of students' learning and achievement. Those in favor of stealth assessment claim that it is a more accurate portrayal of students' day-to-day capabilities anyway (Kamenetz 2015).

In multiple measures the data collected from many sources and angles paints a broader picture of students' abilities and knowledge than data from a single assessment. These data could be collected in longitudinal data systems that track students from prekindergarten all the way through college, and they reflect a big-data approach where information like graduation rates, discipline outcomes, demographic information, teacher-created assessments, and eventually workforce outcomes, all work together to paint a larger picture of each student. This big data from multiple measures could be used to analyze the performance of students, schools, teachers, and communities over time.

Game-based assessments and performance or portfolio-based assessments are also gaining a lot of traction in the world of education. Game-based assessments that take on a video-game feel are likely to be more engaging to students and have the capability of providing them immediate and specific feedback, that is, "You completed this skill and gained this many points, so you can move on to the next level."

Performance-based assessments are already happening in schools across America. They include student projects, presentation, and papers collected over time. Districts that use portfolios and teacher-created assessments as a means of informing their instruction and analyzing student work tend to show higher graduation rates and better college-retention rates than districts that do not (Kamenetz 2015).

Finally, many stakeholders of public education are considering the idea of analyzing students' social and emotional skills through student, teacher, and parent surveys. After all, at least half of students' chances of future success are chalked up to their nonacademic qualities including perseverance, hope, curiosity, etc. Proponents of social/emotional skills survey suggest that these tests should be a part of the multiple measures schools are implementing to assess students' readiness for college and career life as schools should be held accountable for cultivating this half of the picture of readiness as well (Kamenentz 2015).

Sir Ken Robinson (2013), author, speaker, and international advisor on education, is leading the discussion in favor of a different approach, not only to assessment, but also to the system of public education altogether. He argues that NCLB legislation and the obsession with standardized assessment that followed has led to the demotivation of teachers and students, the disinterest in learning, and the enormous dropout rate of America's students.

He states that the irony of NCLB is that it has left so many children behind. In some parts of America, sixty percent of students dropout of high school each year. In the Native American communities the number is as high as eighty percent. He argues that if we cut that number in half, economists estimate that after ten years it would create a net gain to the U.S. economy of nearly a trillion dollars.

In other words, these assessments that are designed to gauge how ready our students are for college and career are actually pushing our students out of school and creating an abhorrence for learning and learning institutions; and instead of these reforms propelling America forward in the global economy they are costing us trillions of dollars (Robinson 2013).

The dropout crisis, though, is only the tip of the iceberg. These numbers do not account for the students who stay in school but are disengaged from it, who do not enjoy it, and who do not see how learning is relevant to their own lives whatsoever. According to the Student Gallup Poll, in 2014, only fifty-three percent of U.S. students were hopeful, only fifty-three percent stated that they are engaged in school, and only sixty-four percent said that they have a positive well-being or are thriving in school and in life (Gallup 2015).

Will more and harder tests change these numbers? It is doubtful. Even for stakeholders who believe that high expectations and accountability are nonnegotiable in schools, they too have to see that accountability and expectations alone do not motivate or inspire students or lead to college and career readiness. Rather, they are only barometers of academic achievement—symptoms of systems that are functioning to inspire students to be hopeful and engaged and meet those high standards.

BACK TO THE BASICS

One consequence of the emphasis on assessment and accountability has been the narrowing of the curriculum. Because the Common Core State Standards only spell out what students should know and be able to do in language arts and math, and because schools and teachers are only held accountable for their students' scores on the assessments that measure their proficiency on these standards, the standards that are assessed often end up being the only standards that are taught.

The irony here is that language arts and mathematics are so important because they are the vehicles of success in so many pursuits in life. The writers of the Common Core knew this and didn't intend for them to be the end goal, but rather the vehicles for teachers of all disciplines to help make their students better communicators and problem solvers (Garland 2014).

The overall focus of language arts can be thought of as the ability to read and listen to understand others and speak and write so others can understand us. Essentially, to master language arts is to master effective communication.

Regardless of one's profession or passion, these skills are necessities. Mathematics can be thought of as the ability to understand patterns and systems in order to tackle problems that deal with numbers, space, and quantity from a variety of angles.

The language arts and mathematics we do outside of school, however, are completely different from the language arts and mathematics that we do inside of school—mostly because what we do inside of school has lost all real-world context. Rather than these disciplines being the vehicles for real-world learning, the learning stops at the skills, concepts, and algorithms defined by the standards.

What's more, all education systems in the world have this hierarchy of subjects with mathematics and the languages at the top, then the humanities and the arts at the bottom. The subjects considered most useful for the workforce and the most indicative of academic ability are at the top, with the whole system being predicated on the most useful skills and knowledge for higher education and the workforce (Robinson 2006).

In other words, our current curriculum is based on backward design of skills and knowledge necessary to enter college and career rather than a system designed on the interests, passion, and engagement of children. The problem with this is that students come to us with a variety of talents and interests and we squander them by taking the variety and interest out of the curriculum.

If, however, we were to design a system around how children flourish, it would look very different and yet likely lead to the same, if not better, readiness for college and careers, and we would leave fewer children behind because schools would be engines of hope, inspiration, and engagement. Human beings, Robinson (2013) asserts, are naturally different and diverse. Yet, current education reform is based on conformity rather than diversity.

Robinson believes that one of the worst symptoms of this conformity is the widespread diagnosis of ADHD in students across America. What should we expect, he asks, if we make small children stay in their seats for hours at a time doing low-grade clerical work? We should be expecting them to fidget. They are kids, after all. They are not suffering from a psychological condition, he states. They are suffering from childhood. One of the reasons they are suffering, though, is because the curriculum is so narrow that it is not tapping into their talents and interests (Robinson 2013).

We just need to look at Finland, the top performing education system in the world, according to the PISA data. Finland has very little standardized testing, and they don't obsess about the disciplines at the top of the hierarchy. Rather, they have a broad approach to education that includes physical education, arts, and the humanities as they know that these are the subjects that often make students come to life—that help students to achieve the state of flow.

Not surprisingly, Finnish schools do not even track their students' dropout rates because there is no need to; there isn't really a dropout rate in Finland (Robinson 2013).

The opposite is true in America. This narrow curriculum is taking its toll—and especially on our boys. According to statistics from the Hundred Girls Project, for every 100 girls who are suspended from school, 250 boys are suspended. For every 100 girls who are expelled from school, 335 boys are expelled (Carr-Chellman 2010).

For every 100 girls receiving a placement in special education because of a learning disability, there are 276 boys, and for every 100 girls diagnosed with emotional disturbance, there are 324 boys. Also, if you are a boy, you are four times more likely to receive a diagnosis of ADHD while you are in school. These numbers are all significantly higher, too, for our boys who also happen to be black (Carr-Chellman 2010).

These patterns remain true even as students get older. Almost seventy percent of college students are now women. These numbers are even starting to make university administrators nervous because with fewer and fewer men attending higher education, they are worried that women will not be as interested in attending colleges that have fewer males in attendance.

College administrators tend to blame the decline in men's attendance on their disengagement with academics because of their obsession with video games and other distractors, but Carr-Chellman counters that these obsessions are merely symptoms of a much larger problem: boys were turned off from school a long time ago. From the time they are in kindergarten, boys are basically told, "Sit down, be quiet, concentrate, do what you're told, be a girl" (Carr-Chellman 2010).

Tony Wagner, former elementary and high school teacher, innovation education fellow at the Technology and Entrepreneurship Center at Harvard University, and founding executive director of Engaging Schools, a Cambridge, Massachusetts, nonprofit, agrees that this narrowing of the curriculum is actually creating a situation where children will have difficulty being innovators later in life. The unfortunate irony is that helping students become future innovators is the exact goal that inspired current education reform (Moran 2014).

Wagner's research, however, revealed that the average child asks 100 questions a day, but by the time a child is ten or twelve, that number decreases exponentially because students are more concerned with getting the answer right than continuing to ask thoughtful questions. So how do we create future innovators? Wagner says that the answer is through allowing play, fostering curiosity, igniting students' passions, rewarding fearlessness, and keeping purpose transparent (Moran 2014).

Many researchers are now suggesting that we should be approaching education less from of an understanding about what students know and can do and more from an understanding about what motivates them. Duckworth (2013), a former educator turned psychologist, found that a significant predictor of students' success is grit, the passion and perseverance for very long-term goals. Duckworth started studying grit in the Chicago Public Schools System by having thousands of students take grit questionnaires and then gathering data to see who would graduate.

Students who demonstrated the most grit on the questionnaires were significantly more likely to graduate than those who didn't, even when factoring in family income, standardized assessment results, and how safe students felt at school (Duckworth 2013). Grit is a symptom though. If grit is passion and perseverance for long-term goals, we cannot simply improve grit by telling students to persevere. We also have to ignite their passions and help them to develop the mind-sets that lead to perseverance.

Dweck's (2006) research provides some insight into how to foster grit in schools. Carol Dweck, Stanford University psychologist, asserts that students' mind-sets are related to their understanding about from where ability comes. Students with fixed mind-sets believe that ability is innate and that their intelligence and talents are fixed traits. Their goal is to avoid risks and look smart. Students with growth mind-sets believe that ability is based on hard work and persistence. They understand that they can get smarter or better at something if they work at it.

These mind-sets have a huge impact on students' success. Students with growth mind-sets are more likely to feel empowered and take on challenging work, whereas students with fixed mind-sets are more likely to feel powerless and demonstrate learned helplessness (Dweck 2006; Jensen 2013). In countries, like Japan, where students consistently perform better than American students on the international PISA assessment, students who did well on the assessment stated that they believe that it was due to all the hard work and effort they put into their studies.

In America, however, the large majority of students attribute their success on the same test to their raw intelligence or talent. Researchers state that one way we can foster growth mind-sets among students is to focus on praising students for their effort rather than their achievement. Yet, educators would likely tell you that this is often the opposite of what happens in schools, especially in this current climate of measurement and accountability through standardized curricula and assessment.

Regardless, it is clear that passion is an integral part of both grit and a growth mind-set. Yet, both students and other stakeholders argue that much of what we teach in schools is not relevant to students' lives in the first place.

The reason is that our focus is on information, achievement, and expertise instead of utility, importance, and interest (Hough 2015). Currently, students are asked to memorize large masses of information that aren't always important to their lives, and are often only remembered for the test and aren't retained in their long-term memories.

Instead of focusing on how to use the information and make it relevant to their lives, students are simply asked to know it with no meaningful end goal in mind. In addition, achievement is emphasized over importance. Students' scores on standardized tests are regarded as signs of success, even if the skills and knowledge being measured aren't important for their futures or their lives.

Finally, expertise, or being placed in AP English or calculus, is considered the pinnacle of student success; yet, we seem to give little care to whether the student is even interested in the discipline or plans to use his learning in the future. Thus, how do we expect students to have grit and growth mind-sets if they don't even care about what they are learning in the first place or see how it is relevant to their lives?

One way to help kids care about their learning is to make the learning fun. And, one tried and true method for infusing fun into learning is through the integration of the arts. Sadly, art is often the first thing to be eliminated when rigorous standards and assessments are introduced despite the fact that ample research points to how arts instruction is correlated with increased math and science scores (Robinson 2013; Schwartz 2015).

One school in Vermont only had seventeen percent of third graders reaching proficiency in math on their New England Common Assessment Program (NECAP) test. However, five years after becoming an arts-integrated magnet school, sixty-six percent of students met or exceeded the standards in math. Moreover, in that same school after the arts were reintroduced, referrals for behavior are almost nonexistent, and students and their families are more engaged in school (Schwartz 2015).

Another way to develop grit and growth mind-sets is through focusing on the executive functioning skills of students. Konnikova (2015) found that there is a distinct correlation between a student's executive functioning skills and her ease in learning how to read. Executive functioning skills include managing time and attention, switching focus from one task to another, planning and staying organized, remembering details, curbing inappropriate speech or behavior, and learning from past experiences. In other words, executive functioning skills are the soft skills of learning.

What Konnikova found through her research was that the students who were able to develop these soft skills from kindergarten through grade three were able to pick up reading skills and develop the foundational skills in literacy that allowed them to be successful later in school and in life. However, the students who were not able to develop these soft skills often were never able to catch up and always struggled with reading.

This finding mimics another study by American psychologist, Walter Mischel, commonly referred to as "The Marshmallow Test." In this test, researchers gave young children a marshmallow and told them that they could eat it if they wanted to, but if they waited a few minutes and didn't eat it, then they would be given another marshmallow. The researchers then tracked the two groups of students (the ones who ate the marshmallow and the ones who waited) over the course of their lives.

What they found was that overwhelmingly, the children who were able to delay their gratification and wait performed better academically, earned more money, were healthier and happier, and were more likely to avoid negative outcomes, including jail time, obesity, and drug use. This delaying of gratification is a symptom of higher executive functioning skills. The good news is that we know how to improve students' executive functioning skills. We just seem to always focus more on the symptoms of poor executive functioning in schools, that is, reading ability, poor behavior, poor academic performance, etc., rather than the soft skills themselves (Konnikova 2015).

These poor executive functioning skills, fixed mind-sets, and negative attitudes regarding education are not only prevalent in our schools but are prevalent in greater society as well. When the 1983 *A Nation at Risk* report announced that our public schools in America were failing, we called in our best management experts in the country to fix the problem.

A generation and a tremendous amount of money later, in many respects we are worse off now than when the report was issued. We have used nearly every tool in the management toolbox and now advisors are reaching desperately in their efforts to find anything that might address the issue. Sadly, their last-ditch management efforts are ranking teachers, firing the lowest-scoring ones, and an endless stream of perpetual testing. This has become the accountability agenda (Walters 2015).

Frustratingly, though, these approaches are the exact opposite of what most leadership and management gurus teach. Although experts in leadership and management agree that data are important, they know that people's attitudes are the key to real change. Management strategies that focus on threatening and firing workers with rationale that they are hurting the bottom line never work to improve organizations.

Rather than trying to fix schools through these last-ditch efforts (that are, in fact, proven horrible organizational management tools), we would do better to focus on the attitudes Americans have about schooling. International studies show that cultures that foster positive attitudes about learning translate to young students' beliefs that learning is essential for success and that with effort and hard work, they can succeed (Walters 2015).

We are currently engaged in an intense chicken and egg debate in America about prevalence of poverty in this country and the quality of our education system. Some state that poor education has led to our widespread poverty, and some state that widespread poverty affects students' ability and readiness to learn in schools. Regardless of which comes first, it is clear that each has an effect on the other.

Additionally, what's even clearer is that current research shows the connection between psychology and the success of our students from low socioeconomic status. In other words, according to the research, the key to closing the achievement gap is not simply raising the standards and giving more assessments but in tapping into the motivation and intrinsic drive of our students (Jensen 2013; Robinson 2013; Walters 2015).

In fact, of the ten major barriers that Walters (2015) studied to explain why low-income students demonstrate low achievement rates, eight of the ten barriers to success were psychological. And, none of these psychological barriers are going to be addressed by higher standards, teacher accountability, constant testing, or narrowing the curriculum.

Fortunately, there are some researchers who are thinking and studying outside the management box in the field of education. Their studies are demonstrating that attitudes are powerful factors in student success and educational achievement. Soft skills like self-efficacy, character, mind-set, grit, and resilience are beginning to be seen as the ticket to tapping into students' full potentials and maximizing their successes.

However, it will be nearly impossible to try to instill these attitudes and work ethics in one student at a time, one family at a time. These traits are not developed at the individual level, but rather are cultivated at a cultural level. Communities hand down these traits and values from elders to youngsters, and absent this larger cultural or system-wide change, change and improvement at the student level will continue to be elusive.

Robinson (2013) argues that public education is not a mechanical system. Rather, it's a human system:

> We have to embrace a different metaphor. We have to recognize that it's a human system, and there are conditions under which people thrive, and conditions under which they don't. We are after all organic creatures, and the culture of the school [and the larger society] is absolutely essential. . . . You take an area, a school, a district, you change the conditions, give people a different sense of possibility, a different set of expectations, a broader range of opportunities, you cherish and value the relationships between teachers and learners, you offer people the discretion to be creative and to innovate in what they do, and schools that were once bereft spring to life (Robinson 2013, 16:12).

Every education reform has a cost and benefit. The minds behind the Common Core movement surely were hopeful that the benefit of this reform would be students who were better prepared for the global economy so that America could maintain its status as a global superpower. The costs of this reform, though, have been the demoralization of educators and students and the risk of America losing its reputation for creativity, entrepreneurship, innovation, and passion—qualities that can be described as "the American spirit."

The problem, however, doesn't lie with the standards or assessments but with districts' and states' decisions to put numbers ahead of students' needs. We do not have to sacrifice rigor to inspire students and help them to care about and enjoy learning. In fact, rigor and challenge are essential to student motivation. The Common Core was not designed with the intention of narrowing the curriculum and watering down the content or at the expense of teaching students the soft skills of learning and being. Nevertheless, that is how it has been translated into practice when leaders', principals', and educators' primary indicator of success is a single data point.

One can argue that these current initiatives were developed reactively (once again) and out of the fear that Americans were falling behind other countries—not only in academics, but in the global economy as well. The emphasis on math and science has again increased as well as the emphasis on literacy that promotes critical thinking and twenty-first-century learning skills.

Prior to the Great Depression, the pendulum of American education had swung all the way to one side with the progressive movement, but the war era began to pull the pendulum back in the other direction. Educators are still riding that pendulum back and forth today—with the fate of the child sitting at one end of the ride and the fate of the country at the other. It is hard, though, to think that these two ends of the spectrum are mutually exclusive. Rather, isn't the fate of our country dependent on the spirit of each child . . . and vice versa?

Likely George Counts, famous American educator and influential education theorist, would say they are. Counts discussed the need to revamp progressive education so that it had a clearly defined purpose—one that benefited the social welfare of our country in addition to the welfare of each child. He stated that progressivism became more about the needs of the upper-middle class to pamper and shelter their children than to engage children in relevant and real-world problem solving. What Counts was advocating in American education was balance between those seemingly opposing ends of the spectrum (Counts 1978).

It makes so much sense. Yet, I'm not sure that we have been able to achieve that balance in our education system in America. What would it look like to have a rigorous, purposeful system of education that propelled America forward as a world leader, promoted collectivism and collaboration in society, *and* fostered the individual growth and spirit of each child through instruction that was relevant to their lives and interests?

Can we simultaneously hold high expectations and promote personal freedom? If we can stop riding the pendulum back and forth long enough to determine for ourselves what the purpose of education really is, then we can proactively create the society we want rather than having society reactively create the education it needs.

Chapter 4

Society's Needs and Values

Our individual narratives become the inspiration behind public policy, and those narratives can be categorized into two broader stories: one of progress and one of decline (Boyle & Burns 2012). The two stories of public schooling in America are no different. One storyline is that public education in America has produced the most creative, innovative citizens our society has ever witnessed.

We are educating more American citizens than ever before and providing them with more skills and knowledge than ever before. Moreover, education is more equitable than ever with traditionally underserved students having more access to the content and instruction than any other time in American history *and* than any other advanced democracy.

Additionally, most parents, while distrustful of the quality of American education as a whole, will tell you that *their* child's public school is in fact quite an amazing place to learn and grow. Most parents are proud of their neighborhood school and believe that it is the exception to the rule in public education. If most parents in America love their own neighborhood schools, then according to the narrative of progress, most schools in America must be okay.

Giving legitimacy to the progress narrative is the fact that about ten years ago, during the dawn of the NCLB movement, government administrators did not release an analysis of the state of American public schools that they themselves had completed because it contradicted the rhetoric of schools in crisis. They did not publish it because if schools were not in crisis like they wanted the American public to believe they were, then they would not be able to push NCLB legislation forward. It was critical that the public felt that public education was in dire straits, and that they had a sense of urgency to make drastic changes (Boyle & Burns 2012).

A recent report from the Economic Policy Institute comparing American public schools to their international peers corroborates this narrative. The report broke down students' PISA (Program for International Student Assessment) scores by socioeconomic status in order to compare apples to apples instead of the usual comparison of apples to oranges. Students in poverty in America were compared to students in poverty from other nations, and affluent students were compared to affluent students from other nations.

What the data revealed was that American students are outstanding readers, and in math our disadvantaged students are growing faster and have improved more than students in almost every country in which the assessment was given. In every country, students from low-income homes score worse than rich students. It just so happens that the United States has a disproportionately large number of students from low-income families.

Thus, the composition of students in the sample that the PISA assessment gathers from America is vastly different from the composition that it collects from other countries (Thompson 2013).

When we even out the variables in the study, we have a better picture of the impact that each country's education system has on students' learning. According to the progress narrative of America's public school system, schools are doing amazingly well, especially considering the uphill battle that many of them face in terms of helping to right society's wrongs.

Conversely, the narrative of decline begins half a century ago with Sputnik. Around the 1960s, public education began to become the scapegoat for America's problems, and the failure narrative took off. According to those who propagated this story, discipline lacked; students and teachers knew that because of social promotion (advancing students to the next grade on the sole basis of age) they did not have to exert much effort or foster any rigor in day-to-day teaching and learning; teachers inflated grades to make it look like students were accomplishing more than they actually were; and the emphasis on multicultural education and teaching the whole child made teaching more fuzzy than focused.

This disaster resulted in the federal government wasting huge amounts of money to take over the whole operation of public education. And, throughout all of these shifts in public education, America has continued to fall further behind in the global marketplace. What's worse, according to those invested in this narrative, amidst all this failure, public schools are and have been accountable to no one. Unions and collective bargaining are largely to blame, and the only way out of this mess is to manage schools more like businesses (Boyle & Burns 2012).

As with most paradoxes, it is possible for these two seemingly contradictory stories to exist simultaneously, and it is even likely that they both speak to an underlying truth about public education. It is possible that American education is both a success story and a cause for concern.

It is likely that our previous philosophies that guided public education have, in fact, created some of the most creative and innovative citizens in the world. It is also possible that at the same time many students have fallen through the cracks, and unfortunately, the systems and individuals that allowed them to fall have not been liable for that devastating oversight. In order to paint a realistic picture of the quality of America's public school system, we must first be clear about the mission our schools are trying to accomplish. How can we gauge our school system's success without first being clear about its end goal?

This brings us to another paradox in education: schooling is both an end in and of itself as well as a means to an end (Boyle & Burns 2012). Learning on its own is a worthy goal to pursue, and yet at the same time, different stakeholders of public education hold different purposes for that learning. And, although it is reasonable to assume that we are clear about what those end goals of public education are, this is not the case. "If we were, public school supporters and reformers would not disagree so vehemently about whether the public education glass is half-empty or half-full" (Boyle & Burns 2012, p. 1).

One thing is certain, however, regardless of the stories we tell, public education in America is a service for the general public and for the future of society. In fact, Boyle and Burns (2012) argue that public education actually has little to do with children. Rather, "schools are political and ideological institutions in which each generation battles among itself for supremacy in determining the purposes, goals, and direction of public education" (p. xiii).

Included in the battles are debates over issues like school lunch, prayer in school, dress code, bilingual education, the extent of freedom of speech in schools, and so on. Public education has always been the battlefield where wars over our country's civic needs, economic needs, and social needs are fought.

CIVIC NEEDS

We educate for a variety of reasons, but a central mission has always been to preserve our democracy. Yet, the founders of America purposefully made it extremely difficult to change our democratic republic, and since trying to change schools is really about trying to change American society, we are often faced with the realization that we are not making much ground (Boyle & Burns 2012).

Because the task is so ambiguous at best (considering we are not clear about our most important mission in public education) and seemingly insurmountable at worst (with the overwhelming charge of changing society as a whole), we often resort to attractive silver bullets of education reform: quick fixes and one-size-fits-all initiatives. Yet, none of these reforms have been the silver bullet of school and societal improvement, and none will ever be if we do not broaden our vision and the subsequent reforms for public education.

It is almost impossible to use public education in America to sustain and improve our democracy because democracy itself is not an easily defined entity. Thus, we resort to preparing students for democratic life simply by encouraging civic responsibility. So, what is civic responsibility? What does being a good citizen entail? According to Carpini (2000), citizenship has taken on various definitions depending on which era of American history one examines.

In the first era—the eighteenth and early nineteenth centuries—citizenship was mostly defined by the extent to which Americans deferred to the political elites. In other words, being a good citizen meant being in step with the ideals and requests of the government at the time. Throughout the remainder of the nineteenth century, one's civic duties meant playing a more central role in the democracy—where one's involvement strengthened the political parties and helped to move the masses.

In the early twentieth century, civic duty took on yet another connotation. Respecting the expertise of government officials and expecting managerial efficiency characterized good citizens of this era. Finally, from the second half of the twentieth century to today, being a good citizen was synonymous with being aware of and promoting the rights of individuals and groups in America (Caprini 2000).

While defining democracy and citizenship is challenging, we can attempt to boil our democracy down to a list of attributes citizens must possess in order to preserve and uphold America's ideals. Attributes might include open mindedness to others' opinions and a willingness to listen to others' points of view; respect for worldviews and values that differ from one's own; treating others justly regardless of their background and values; and a commitment to discuss issues, reason with others, and deliberate, debate, and struggle to find a compromise when issues arise.

Certainly there is value to these civic aims. How many politicians in American society today exemplify these traits? How many citizens demonstrate these ideals? Tackling civic issues in public schools means ensuring the curriculum brings together diverse students and asks them to live and work using these same democratic ideals where their diversity is valued rather than used to sort and select students to determine who will live a privileged life and who will not.

Society's Needs and Values

We need to ensure that the content that is taught in schools is relevant and significant to both students and society in order to prepare them for living out the democratic ideals we cherish. So are we succeeding at fostering our civic goals in schools? Some argue that these attributes of civic-minded students are arguably strongly promoted in the Common Core with standards such as

- Write arguments to support claims in an analysis of substantive topics or texts, using valid reasoning and relevant and sufficient evidence;
- Initiate and participate effectively in a range of collaborative discussions . . . with diverse partners . . . on topics, texts, and issues, building on others' ideas and expressing their own clearly and persuasively;
- Delineate and evaluate the argument and specific claims in a text, assessing whether the reasoning is sound and the evidence is relevant and sufficient; recognize when irrelevant evidence is introduced;
- Delineate a speaker's argument and specific claims, evaluating the soundness of the reasoning and relevance and sufficiency of the evidence and identifying when irrelevant evidence is introduced;
- Gather relevant information from multiple print and digital sources. . .; assess the credibility and accuracy of each source;
- Analyze the purpose of information presented in diverse media and formats . . . and evaluate the motives (e.g., social, commercial, political) behind its presentation; and
- Analyze seminal U.S. documents of historical and literary significance (e.g., Washington's Farewell Address, the Gettysburg Address, Roosevelt's Four Freedoms speech, King's "Letter from Birmingham Jail"), including how they address related themes and concepts.

Will these standards eventually lead to civic responsibility? Will they alone meet our civic goals in education? The writers of the Common Core believe they will. Yet, the emphasis we place on our civic ideals in schools pales in comparison to emphasis we place on our economic desires.

ECONOMIC NEEDS

Although some scholars argue that the purpose of public education should be to promote the values that will sustain the democratic republic, in recent years, U.S. governors undeniably contend that public education exists for economic purposes more than any other. Carpenter and Hughes (2011) headed a study where they codified the language that U.S. governors used when speaking about public education's purpose.

Their findings were revealing. Over sixty-two percent of the phrases they used when speaking about education implied that the purpose of education was to sustain and improve the economy. Twenty-five percent of the phrases had to do with improving students' self-regulation and human relationships, a little over seven percent hinted at civic responsibility but were not overt, and a little under four percent mentioned that schools should focus on human relationships. It seems that in recent times, the primary focus of schools has gone from preserving our democracy to stimulating our economy.

While U.S. governors are chiefly concerned with using schools as tools to improve our country's economy, business leaders in America argue that doing so requires schools to focus on the soft skills of employment more so than the technical and academic skills. When interviewed about the deficits employers are seeing in their workers, sixty-nine percent of business leaders cited issues with work ethic, including attendance, timeliness, and effort; and thirty-four percent discussed insufficient work experience (Spring 2008). Note that the top two concerns did not even relate to skills in literacy or math, which are arguable the two primary foci of what we measure in public schools.

The third greatest concern of employers was lack of reading and writing skills (thirty-two percent mentioned this), and twenty-seven percent of employers mentioned workers not passing drug screenings. Poor references from previous employers was mentioned by twenty-percent of the employers, and inadequate oral communication skills was next on the list with eighteen percent of employers citing it as a problem.

In addition, twelve percent of employers stated their concern that workers were not able to work in a team environment. And, finishing up the list of issues that the smallest percentage of employers stated as concerns were inadequate problem solving skills, inadequate computer and/or technical skills, lack of degree or vocation training, and problems with citizenship/immigration (Spring 2008).

Why then, if employers did not even mention math or science skills in their list of concerns, and why, if literacy was not even at the top of their list, do we continue to focus in schools solely on math, science, and literacy as the means of improving the economy? Politicians will tell you that it is because we are preparing students for jobs of the future—jobs that do not even currently exist. And, jobs of the future, they say, will require higher academic and technical skill than ever before. Does that mean, however, that concerns about work ethic and social skills will simply disappear as students' academic skills increase?

Another relevant issue regarding the economic purposes for education is the inflation of college degrees. According to UESCO, United Nations Educational, Scientific, and Cultural Organization, in the next thirty years, more people worldwide will be earning college degrees than ever before. On one hand, we are saying that higher education is necessary for American students to obtain in order for the United States to remain competitive in the global economy. On the other hand, many worry that degrees are going to become worthless because now one needs a PhD for jobs that previously required an MA, an MA for jobs that previously required a BA, and a BA for jobs that previously required a high school diploma.

Bill Gates argues that education is the ticket to prosperity because the current U.S. economy only provides the best opportunities to those with the best education. Thus, we have to focus on providing equal opportunity for all students in America to attend institutions of higher education. He states that this is necessary in order for the United States to remain economically strong and remain the leaders of the pack in the fields of math and science.

The real economic crisis, he says, stems from the fact that over thirty percent of our students never finish high school and for minority students the statistics are over fifty percent. Sadly, even if students do graduate from high school, if they are low-income students, their chances of ever acquiring a college degree are less than twenty-five percent. If a student is from the low-income group in the United States, he has a higher chance of going to jail than he does of obtaining a four-year degree, and that, he states, is the fault of our public education system (Gates 2009).

I doubt there are many people who would argue with the idea that the disparities in opportunities that our low-income students face in contrast to our affluent students are real rather than illusion. However, there are disagreements about the root causes of those disparities. While Gates urges American schools to increase their rigor and opportunities in academics for our impoverished students, others push for an increased focus on engagement and students' well-being.

SOCIAL NEEDS

Many argue that the primary reason for the dropout crisis in America is not solely academic but is largely attributed to the fact that we do not address the toxic stress or learned helplessness that many students in poverty bring to school each day. In the United States today, twenty-three percent of our students live in poverty. In Finland that figure is almost five times smaller (Strauss 2013).

In light of these statistics, it is no coincidence that Finnish schools are considered the best in the world, far outpacing the United States. It is also likely no coincidence that American students recently ranked in the bottom four on child well-being according to a recent United Nations review. The sad reality is that among twenty-nine wealthy countries, the United States is second from the last in child poverty and just as low in "child life satisfaction" (Strauss 2013).

Poverty is not just an economic issue. It is a social issue as well. Even if we hold the acquisition of money and power as our ultimate purpose for public education in America, knowledge and skills alone will not unlock the potential of our students to obtain them. Knowledge and skill alone will not increase students' life satisfaction or well-being.

Without addressing the social and emotional symptoms of poverty in our schools we will not equip our students with the tools they need to live productive and successful lives. Without addressing these social and emotional symptoms in schools, we will never address the equity issues between the privileged and the disadvantaged in public education and society.

It's not only students from poverty, however, who require more than just their academic needs met in order to reach their full potential. A recent Gallup Poll of students in the United States attempted to measure students' levels of hope, engagement in school, and general well-being. The results were heartbreaking. Only fifty-three percent of students were found to be hopeful, sixty-four percent were found to have a positive well-being, and only fifty-three percent claimed to find school engaging.

For those who see public education as the means for improvement in our global economy, the real devastation of this study is that these three factors have been shown to drive students' grades, achievement scores, retention, and future employment (Gallup 2015). Regardless of our individual desires for public education and for students, the fact is that according to this study, nearly half of the students in American schools are suffering, and yet we are doing next to nothing in terms of federal or state reforms to address or even acknowledge this suffering.

The lowest scores in the poll were around statements regarding school safety and students' feelings of significance and importance. These sad statistics are turning into even sadder realities in many of our public schools. It has been three years since twenty-year-old Adam Lanza shot his way into Sandy Hook Elementary School in Newtown, Connecticut, and killed twenty first-grade students, six staff members, and himself, resulting in the deadliest mass shooting at a public school in U.S. history.

This incident spurred a nationwide debate on gun control and mental health issues, but discussions on the implications for schools (other than school safety) seemed to get much less attention. Recently, however, a team of doctors, lawyers, educators, and social workers from Connecticut's Office of the Child Advocate issued a report stating that while Lanza was solely to blame for the incident, there were also warning signs that were ignored and opportunities to intervene were missed throughout his life and schooling (Cohen 2014).

The report indicated that a large concern of the team was the lack of training, knowledge, and expertise on the part of the adults in Lanza's life regarding his social and emotional state throughout his school experience. His mother, overwhelmed with his deficits and needs, had the goal to simply manage and get through each day. Additionally, she was able to convince the staff of the schools he attended to accommodate and appease her son by avoiding things that made him feel uncomfortable.

Sarah Eagan, one of the authors of the report and the state's child advocate, stated that by the time Lanza began high school, the school administration had only one goal for him: to keep him moving forward academically—to help him graduate. They were maintaining a focus on what they believed to be the most important aspect of Lanza's growth. The report stated that the district was happy as long as Lanza was enrolled in and earning the amount of credits he would need to graduate.

The school was less concerned and largely ignored entirely his social and emotional development. They focused only on his academic development at the expense of addressing his psychological demons. He totally slid under their radar despite his obvious and serious social and emotional needs (Cohen 2014). One might deduce that the school's sole interest in Lanza was as a data point.

Eagan stated that this would be horrible enough as an isolated incident, but this oversight of students' social and emotional needs has become more of the rule than the exception. The reason that it has become a problem, she states, is because (a) it is expensive to get students the help they need and (b) it is not the priority in education.

As long as the federal purpose for education is competing in the global economy and as long as districts' purposes in education are compiling good data in order to look good and receive more funding, we are in danger of positioning ourselves to be susceptible to more tragedies like the one at Sandy Hook. By ignoring what children need in order to develop properly, we are not only keeping them from realizing their potential and purpose in life, but we are also putting them and ourselves in harm's way. We are entirely discounting and disregarding students' social and emotional needs.

The disturbing irony here is that social and emotional well-being is the key to personal power, fulfillment, and future success. Anthony Robbins, self-help author, speaker, and peak performance coach, has spent decades analyzing why people do what they do—why they sometimes succeed and why they sometimes fail—and he has come to the conclusion that activating individuals' internal drive is the most important thing we can do in the world. (If it is true that it is the most important thing we can do in the world, then shouldn't it be true that it is also the most important thing we can do in education?)

He further argues that emotion is the key to unlocking this internal drive. Robbins (2006) states that if we can improve where we are at emotionally, then we can contribute more, have more empathy for others, and create the kinds of ideas and connections that can fix some of our biggest challenges in society today. Robbins argues that what makes or breaks the quality of an individual's life boils down to two lessons and whether or not the individual masters those lessons.

The first lesson is the science of achievement: what you need to know and the skills you need to master in order to reach your end goal. This is the lens through which public schools attempt to breed success, and this is the lesson that is easiest for most individuals to master.

The second lesson, though, is the art of fulfillment, which is rarely mastered by the public (and rarely fostered in public schools). Robbins suggests that the reason that the art of fulfillment is elusive to many is because it is an art—it's not as tangible as the skills, knowledge, and resources that make up the science of achievement. The art of fulfillment is all about the ability to put oneself in a prime emotional state.

Robbins goes on to state that we can put ourselves in a prime emotional state by being cognizant of our decisions. What we decide to focus on and what meaning we give that upon which we have chosen to focus are what produce emotion. For example, if we face a setback in life and focus on how we are a victim of our circumstances, that decision will produce a much different emotion than if we face a setback and choose to focus on how we can use that obstacle to grow, learn, and help others.

That emotion then drives our action. The former meaning that we gave in to our setback—that we are a victim—likely produces emotions of despair and hopelessness. The latter meaning—that we can take our situation and turn it into an opportunity to help others—likely produces emotions of gratitude and hopefulness. Peeling the layers of internal drive and emotional well-being back even further, we find six basic human needs. The degree to which these needs are met influences our decisions and subsequently determines our emotional well-being (Robbins 2006).

The first basic human need, according to Robbins, is certainty. Everybody requires a certain level of certainty that they will be able to be comfortable in life and avoid extreme pain. We might gain certainty through an established routine, a stable salary, and stable relationships. The second need is uncertainty. Everyone also needs a little interest in life. Events and circumstances cannot be totally predictable or life would lack the surprises—the ups and downs—that make it exciting.

So, while we might say that we hate drama, most of us need our problems in life—as long as they do not feel too overwhelming—as they provide a little bit of excitement or uncertainty. The third basic human need is significance.

Every human on the planet desires to feel important and special—that they have worth and they matter. Some people do this by making a lot of money; some people do it by becoming more spiritual; some people do this with their self-expression through fashion or their hobbies and interests. The fastest way to do this, however, is through violence (Robbins 2006).

According to Robbins, if someone puts a gun to another's head, the significance they experience is off the charts. In addition, his certainty need is fulfilled. He is certain that his decision is going to get a reaction or response. And, his uncertainty need is fulfilled. He has no idea what is going to happen next. His life just got a whole lot more interesting.

Robbins asserts that is why violence has always been around and will always be around unless we have a large-scale change in human consciousness. It is hard not to make the leap between these first three basic needs and the events at Sandy Hook Elementary School. It is hard not to wonder if the schools and larger American society had put more of an emphasis on meeting Lanza's basic emotional needs, whether or not the events that transpired could have been avoided.

We cannot blame the schools and society for Lanza's actions. We cannot know that his decisions would have been any different had more adults intervened to improve his social and emotional well-being. But, we can and should use this horrific event as a reason for reflection on how our purpose for public schools impacts the actions we do and do not take on behalf of children.

The fourth basic human need is connection and love. We can achieve this through friendship, intimacy, prayer, and being in nature, but regardless of how we achieve it, we all need it. People who do not have this need fulfilled often engage in unhealthy sexual behavior, affiliate themselves with gangs, etc., in order to meet this desire of connection. These first four needs are all needs of the personality. According to Robbins, every single human on earth finds a way to meet these needs regardless of who they are or from where they come.

The last two human needs, however, are needs of the spirit, and true fulfillment comes from having these two needs met. The first of these last two prerequisites for fulfillment is the need for personal growth. Anyone who isn't growing feels stuck. It is in our nature to learn, grow, and move forward in life. Everyone has the desire to grow because everyone wants to eventually have something of value to give.

This leads us to the last human need: to contribute beyond ourselves. Those who are the happiest and most fulfilled in life are the people who have made a real difference in someone else's life. Contribution to others gives our life purpose. These six needs drive the motivation behind each decision that we make. Whichever need is not being met, or whatever need is our dominant need, becomes our target in life.

Once we have that target, we then move in a direction or make a decision in order to meet it. However, we all have different maps for how we get there—how we arrive at meeting that need. Two people may have the same target of feeling significant. One may choose to enter a service profession such as teaching, law enforcement, or the clergy in order to make a difference in the lives of others, and the other may choose to take someone's life with violence in order to feel important (Robbins 2006).

In fact, Philip Zimbardo, professor emeritus at Stanford University and psychologist famous for his Stanford prison experiment, suggests that we are all capable of good and evil, and it is simply the situation or circumstance that we are in that brings the good or evil out in us. He calls his theory the Lucifer Effect, and he developed it as a result of the Stanford prison study: a study of the power of institutions to influence individuals' behavior. He wanted to see what would transpire when he took ordinary young adults and put them in an environment that pressured them to carry out immoral acts.

Seventy-five college students volunteered to take part in the study; they took personality tests and participated in interviews, and twenty-four were picked who were determined to be the most normal and most healthy. Of those twenty-four, twelve were randomly chosen to be the prisoners in the simulation, and twelve were chosen to be the prison guards. Within five days, the experiment had to be stopped because the guards were dehumanizing the prisoners by physically, mentally, emotionally, and sexually abusing them to the extent that they were no longer safe in the parameters of the experiment (Zimbardo 2008).

Disturbingly, this simulation is not an isolated incident of otherwise normal and healthy individuals committing atrocities because of environmental or social influences. The Milgram experiment is another study that measured the willingness of participants to do evil in spite of their solid ethical foundations. In the study, researchers wanted to see if participants would obey authority figures who were asking them to inflict pain on others despite the participants' moral objections.

In this experiment researchers told participants that their job was to teach another participant—the learner (an actor)—something that the learner was then required to remember. If the teacher asked the learner a question and he got it right, the teacher was told to reward him. However, if the learner did not get the question right, the teacher was to press a button on a box and was told that the button would shock the learner. The first time the teacher pressed the button, they were told it was only fifteen volts, which they were told the learner didn't even feel.

However, the voltage increased with each wrong answer the learner gave. By the end of the experiment the shock was 450 volts, and the button said, "Danger. Severe Shock." However, if participants questioned the experimenter about whether or not they should be pushing the button, the experimenter would say that it was alright because he would be responsible if anything should happen to the person receiving the shock.

Prior to the experiment's completion, forty psychiatrists were asked to predict how many participants would go all the way to 450 volts based on what they knew about human behavior. The psychiatrists were in agreement that only one percent of the participants would hit the 450-volt button because only one percent of the population is thought to be sadistic. The reality, however, was that two-thirds of the participants carried the experiment through all the way to the last button regardless of the fact that they knew better and had reservations (Zimbardo 2008).

It has not only been experiments, however, that point to the capability of humans to do evil given the right circumstances and environment. In 2003, American soldiers earned international notoriety for the torture and abuse of prisoners in Abu Ghraib prison in Iraq. While government administration and military officials blamed it on the prison guards, alluding to the fact that they were simply bad apples, Zimbardo (2008) has a different hypothesis. He believes that American soldiers are mostly good, and that it likely wasn't the apple that was bad, but the barrel.

In other words, it is the system that brings out the good or evil in its people; it is not the good or evil in the people that tarnishes the system. Zimbardo states that if you want to change people, you have to change the situations and systems in which they live and operate. He is careful, though, to make it clear that understanding this phenomenon is not excusing it. It is, however, our responsibility to understand how systems can influence people so that we can improve the systems in which people operate—especially the systems that are designed to have a large influence on society.

So what does all of this have to do with the social needs of American citizens? What does it have to do with our public schools? If it is true that all humans have six basic needs that we will try to meet through whatever means necessary, and if it is true that under certain circumstances humans can do both good and evil—that we can reach our full potential and contribute positively to society or be unaware of our potential and do harm—then it must also be true that we have a responsibility in society to meet each other's basic needs, and we have a responsibility to set up systems that promote fulfillment.

Public schools are an obvious place to start. Do our school systems aim to fulfill students so that they can contribute to society, or do our school systems foster psychological distress? Are the students in our schools primed to achieve or primed to drop out? To be fulfilled or hopeless? To do good or evil?

A recent large-scale survey found that the emotional well-being of college students has fallen to the lowest levels in twenty-five years. Half the college students surveyed reported feeling hopeless, and a third reported feeling so depressed that it is difficult for them to function. Many reported feeling stressed out, empty, anxious, and aimless (Deresiewicz 2014). Unfortunately, this sad state of affairs isn't surprising as it reflects the statistics on the well-being of our kindergarten through twelfth-grade students as well (Gallup 2015).

It is doubtful that this is what is meant by college and career readiness, however. What is the point of academic readiness if we end up sending our students off to college to be hopeless, depressed, and stressed out? Moreover, those statistics only reflect the college students who were surveyed. Imagine the levels of well-being of our students who do not attend college or drop out of high school.

The unfortunate reality is that our school system is more famous for preparing our students for prison than it is for professionalism, illustrated by the recently coined term, "the school-to-prison pipeline." The school-to-prison pipeline refers to the practice of pushing children out of schools and toward the juvenile and criminal justice systems.

Zero tolerance policies, the presence of police officers in many schools, budget cuts that reduce the availability of school counselors, and teachers and principals who are stressed out about the influx of testing and accountability measures simply fuel this trend. All of these practices have led to the increase in student suspensions, expulsions, and arrests of many millions of students—especially minority students (Flannery 2015).

It's not only our minority students and students of poverty who are being channeled into undesirable states of being. Surprisingly, our preteens from affluent and educated families are the ones who experience some of the highest rates of distress of any subgroup in this country. Their rates of depression, drug use, anxiety disorders, and unhappiness are off the charts.

Deresiewicz (2015) claims that this is due to the fact that this generation of students has been conditioned to think that everything they do is for the purpose of looking good in the eyes of others, whether those "others" are college admissions officers, employers, friends on social media, etc. This emptiness caused by lack of being intrinsically driven by an inspiring purpose is what leads to this pervasive unhappiness among precollege and college students alike and eventually leads to the hookups, drugs, and drama we see among many adolescents in their attempt to fill this emptiness.

In fact, a new theory on the cause of drug addiction has shined a light on the extent to which our emotional well-being is essential to our success and fulfillment. Research over the last fifty years suggests that there is a strong case for the notion that the cause of addiction is not what we think it is. The new theory is that addiction is routed in our emotional state. And that emotional state is caused by our environment and contributes to addiction more so than the chemical state caused by the drug.

In the 1980s, the Partnership for a Drug-Free America created a famous advertisement based on a well-known rat experiment. In the experiment researchers put a rat in a cage with two water bottles. In one bottle was just water, and in the other one was water laced with heroin or cocaine. Nearly every time the experiment was ran, the rat would become addicted to the drugged water and continue to come back for more until it overdosed and killed itself (Hari 2015).

In the 1970s, psychology professor Bruce Alexander decided to try the same experiment but in the context of a different environment. In the first experiment, the rat was alone in the cage and had nothing to do except take the drugs. In the second experiment, the researcher created a luxurious environment for the rats and added more rats to the mix so that they were not alone in the cage. He called it Rat Park.

Initially, all the rats tried the two different water bottles not knowing what was in them, but ultimately, in this new experiment, the rats that were living good lives in Rat Park, surrounded by companions and an optimum environment, opted for the water that wasn't laced with drugs. There were still some rats that chose the water laced with drugs every now and then, but none of them became heavy users, and none of them died (Hari 2015).

Hari (2015) suggests the human equivalent of this experiment was taking place at the same time as the rat experiment: the Vietnam War. During the Vietnam War, heroin use among U.S. soldiers was common. In fact, twenty percent of soldiers had become addicted to it during the war. Although the statistics were so frightening that the American public was scared to find out what was going to happen when they returned home, ninety-five percent of the addicted soldiers simply stopped using once they returned from war—the majority without rehab. Hari argues that this is because they transitioned from a hostile cage to a pleasant one.

According to Professor Alexander, this finding challenges both the right wing view—that addiction is a result of weak morals—and the left wing view—that addiction is a disease over which the drug has sole control. After his initial Rat Park experiment, he decided to replicate the experiment in which the rats were left alone in the cage. Again, they became addicted and compulsive users. He left them in the cage and let them use for fifty-seven days until the use nearly killed them.

Then, he took them out of isolation and put them in the plush environment of Rat Park with other rats. He wanted to see if the drugs had such a chemical hold of the rats' brains that they wouldn't be able to stop using. What happened was surprising. Aside from the rats temporarily going through withdrawals, they soon stopped drinking the heroin-laced water and went on to have normal lives (Hari 2015).

The results should not really be that perplexing according to Hari (2015). After all, he states, most people who, for months on end, have to take prescription drugs for pain that basically have the same chemical composition of heroin, never become addicted. Most simply stop once the prescription is no longer needed for their ailment.

This phenomenon, paired with the fact that there are plenty of addictions, such as gambling addiction, sex addiction, and others that are not related to any sort of chemical the user is ingesting, indicate that there is more going on with addiction than just a chemical dependence. Hari states that the antithesis of addiction is not sobriety, but rather it is fulfillment.

If addressing our social downfalls in America is a priority, then looking to public education as one means of addressing those downfalls makes sense. If we see education as a tool that is to improve our social issues in America, then we need to imagine how we can use public education to combat poverty, incarceration, drug addiction, etc. We need to imagine how we might tackle these enormous concerns by attempting to understand the root cause of these matters.

We are currently attempting to address these matters through increasing students' academic achievement. The school-to-prison pipeline is a concern of most stakeholders and the initiator of many of our reforms in public education. Reformers of public education look at the link between preschool attendance and success in their K–12 education and beyond.

They cite the link between students' third grade reading scores and their likelihood of being incarcerated later in life. They discuss the need for a plan and a sense of urgency in making early childhood education more equitable between the haves and have-nots and ensuring that we intervene in literacy long before students fail to read well in third grade (Gates 2010).

Of course these are noble pursuits. Early childhood education is extremely important, and we should work to ensure that all social classes have access to early education for their children. Early literacy is important. Literacy is essential to life in the twenty-first century as well as students' confidence and sense of mastery. Without solid literacy skills, students struggle in nearly every other discipline they encounter, and that struggle has a drastic effect on their well-being, engagement, and hope for the future (Konnikova 2015).

Are we to assume, however, that the link between early childhood education and future success . . . or third grade reading scores and future incarceration rates is causal? It is often assumed that it is—that the academic bridge from preschool to elementary school is the leg up that leads to future success. Could it be, however, that the same parents who send their children to preschool—regardless of their social or economic status—are likely also the parents who possess the skill set that results in many other choices that are in the best interest of their child?

Could it be that most students who are succeeding at reading in third grade are also the same students who are not coming to school with toxic stress from living in an unstable and unhealthy environment? In other words, is a parent who sends his child to preschool also more likely to fulfill his child's social and emotional needs at each stage of her development?

Is it more likely that *most* (not all, of course) high school and college graduates can attribute their success to the foundational knowledge and skills they gained in preschool, or is it more likely that most high school and college graduates can attribute their success to parents and mentors who had the tools to and/or were committed to laying a solid foundation for their children and that preschool attendance and third grade reading scores are *also a symptom* of this greater issue rather than the cause in and of itself?

This is not to say that parents are fully responsible for students' success in school. Teachers, as we have established, have a profound effect on student achievement. However, we must recognize how students' relationships and social/emotional development impact their school and future success if we are to address those relationships and social/emotional well-being in schools. Teachers have long known that the struggles they face in the classroom are a mirror of the social struggles that we face as a society as much as they are about academic abilities.

Poverty is not merely an economic issue, and criminal behavior is not solely a moral issue. There is an academic component to the social issues we face in society, of course. Knowledge is power, after all. But, there is also an emotional component to the social issues that we face, and many argue that it is the stronger influence (Achor 2011; Ariely 2012; Deresiewicz 2014; Gallup Education 2015; Gardner 2014; Goleman 2012; Hari 2015; Jensen 2013; Robbins 2013; Robinson 2013).

If improving our emotional well-being and acquiring the soft skills to make solid decisions are the key to both fulfillment and success, then it would make sense that we include these goals in the purpose of public education. Many students are entering school having experienced unspeakable early trauma and harboring levels of toxic stress that would debilitate most adults.

And yet, in spite of this truth, we tell ourselves that these things are beyond our control. We cross our fingers and hope that the plight that most of our students face does not do too much damage, and we trudge ahead turning a blind eye to their troubles, maintaining our laser-like focus on standards that feel irrelevant to the needs they are aching we meet in false hope that by doing so our issues as a nation will someday be resolved and prosperity will be ours.

Although our social aims have largely fallen by the wayside to our economic desires, that has not always been the case in public education. Carpenter

(2011) states that, historically, the main social aims for public schools can be classified into two categories: goals around self-realization and goals around human relationships. To address self-realization goals, educators worked to develop students' curiosity and creativity *in addition to* their abilities.

Carpenter asserts that these efforts develop the spirit of the student as well as her understanding of her place in the community. This self-realization then equips the student to function more adeptly in not only her social sphere, but in her political and economic sphere as well. However, it is more of a cycle than a linear trajectory as once this student is functioning effectively in all of these spheres, her sense of self and confidence is once again heightened and the process continues.

To address goals around human relationships, schools looked to mitigate the tensions that arise in the battle between individual freedom and social equality. This tension is eased through acquiring a respect for justice, obtaining an awareness of our social ideals as well as social reality, and by developing an understanding of our shared human experience and the human condition (Carpenter 2011). In other words, schools worked to help students find a balance between being autonomous and being a contributing member to the greater good—skills that would be invaluable later in life in the social, political, and economic spheres in which they would operate.

To what extent do we currently focus on self-realization or human relationships under current education policy and reform? As of late, our actions seem to indicate that we care more about and put more of an emphasis on whether or not learning is occurring than what we want students to learn and why we want them to learn it. As long as our measures of achievement indicate that students are academically proficient, we assume that we are successful in our mission even if the student who received the high scores is uninspired, apathetic, and not respectful to or responsible in the school and greater community.

This is in contrast to curricular frameworks in other countries, such as Scotland, which specify that the purpose of education is to develop four capacities in students: that of the successful learner, the confident individual, the responsible citizen, and the effective contributor. Scottish policymakers must understand the interconnectedness of our social, economic, and civic aims. It is time that we honor that interconnectedness in America.

WHAT THE PUBLIC WANTS

When we think of the public that public education is tasked to serve, we often think of community members, parents, and students. Yet, it was not community members, parents, or students who decided on the public school mission of helping U.S. businesses compete in the global economy. Ironically, it was not even community members, parents, or students who led the charge of closing the achievement gap between low-income and minority students and their peers.

Rather, these decisions are made by complex political processes, which are designed to represent the public interests. It is, however, worthwhile to invest in the unique needs and hopes of individual stakeholders and various stakeholder groups because they are the ones who operate in the trenches of the public school system, and without their buy-in the promise of our public schools stops at the steps of the capital building.

Families' Desires

Let us begin by looking at the desires of our public school students. Largely, what students want most from their education is engagement. Essentially, they don't want to be bored. In fact, engagement in school is the number one reason that students choose to stay in school. This is especially true for students living in poverty (Gallup 2015; Jensen 2013). Unfortunately, many of our students are disengaged from school.

In one large-scale survey by Yazzie-Mintz (2007), only two percent of high school students said they were never bored. Over thirty percent of the students said that they did not have day-to-day interactions with their teachers (that would foster personal relationships and increase engagement), and seventy-five percent said that school was not interesting or relevant to their lives. According to Shernoff, Csiksquentmihalyi, Scheider, and Shernoff (2003), the average high school student spends twenty-five percent of her day in a state of complete apathy.

Yet another study found that students as young as fifth grade spent over ninety-percent of their time listening to teachers lecture or working silently and independently at their desks despite their preference for hands on and collaborative learning activities. And, sadly, our students from poverty are the least likely to receive engaging instruction and curriculum (Pianta et al. 2007).

Engagement refers to students' enthusiasm for school—it is the intrinsic investment and effort in learning; and student engagement is the number one difference between low-performing schools and high-performing schools (Gallup 2015). However, there are many factors that contribute to engagement beyond simply a student's interest in the subject matter.

A student's sense of belongingness, her feeling of competence, the amount of autonomy she has, and the meaningfulness of her learning all factor into her level of engagement. Competence, autonomy, and meaningfulness as drivers of intrinsic motivation are themes that have been discussed by Pink

(2011) when he points to the will-drivers of mastery (competence), purpose (meaningfulness), and autonomy, as well. Students, it seems, are no different from employees when it comes to what inspires them to harness their passion and pursue their purpose.

Students feel a sense of belonging if the culture of the school is one that seems to care about their positive well-being. Schools can foster this type of culture by having frequent personal interactions that nurture a mutual respect between students and staff. Competence can be achieved by ensuring that the tasks students are asked to complete in classrooms are not only challenging but also scaffolded by the teacher so that students have the ability to attain the skills and acquire the concepts. Further, continual feedback from the teacher and an environment where mistakes are not only allowed but also encouraged is crucial for promoting competence.

Students feel autonomous when they have choice in their learning and are able to take initiative in pursuing their interests. Educators can foster this by allowing multiple viewpoints, using language that is not geared at controlling their students, allowing for free expression and debate, and encouraging students to ask a lot of questions. Finally, students feel like the learning is meaningful when they see how it is relevant to their lives and their futures.

Teachers can increase students' sense of purpose and make the learning meaningful by building on their background knowledge, drawing on common human experiences as the context for the learning, and by using concrete objects and experiences to enhance the learning. Students want more than just to be engaged in the learning, though. They want to be happy and hopeful as well. Students are not motivated by simply knowing that they will someday have the skills and knowledge to be ready for college life and the workforce. They want to be happy now.

It is not just what they want, but it is what we, the public, should want for them as well. How happy a student is now is a solid predictor for how successful s/he will be in the future (Achor 2011; Gallup Education 2015). According to the 2014 Student Gallup Poll, thirty-four percent of our students in America say they are struggling emotionally, and two percent say that they are suffering (Gallup Education 2015).

Achor (2011) argues that we need to reverse the formula for happiness and success in schools. The current motto is, "Work harder and you will become more successful. When you are successful you will finally be happy." He suggests that instead we should focus on positivity in the present so that students have the "happiness advantage." Because of the increased dopamine, the learning centers in the brain will be turned on, which will lead to greater intelligence, more creativity, and an increase in energy . . . all of which result in better outcomes for students and society.

Part of being happy in the now, however, is being hopeful about one's future. Students' levels of hope are larger predictors of college success than their SAT scores or high school GPA. Only fifty-three percent of U.S. students, though, state that they are hopeful. A staggering thirty-three percent said that they are "stuck," and fourteen percent claim that they are discouraged when they think about their future (Gallup Education 2015).

If you look at these three factors that students desire from their schools—engagement, happiness, and hope—one might conclude that students' desired purpose for schools is to be inspired to learn and grow and to find joy in doing so. Apparently, students do not care too much about the global economy. What about parents? As voters, surely their desires have been taken into account as policymakers have developed and pushed their latest reforms forward. It turns out, though, that their desires are not too different from their children's.

Parent choice has been a hot topic recently in the discussion on equity and opportunity in education. Currently in the United States, some of the most advantaged students have the best access to a quality education, and some of our most disadvantaged students in America have the worst access (Sillers 2015). One would think that a primary goal of parents would be to choose their child's school on the basis of which schools provide the best education—the most rigorous academic curriculum and instruction.

However, in a recent study, when asked about what schools they would choose for their children if given the option, the majority of public school parents would not pick schools based on academic criteria. In fact, the study concluded that parents do not care about academics as much as they say they do.

Rather parents cared more about whether the school was in the community in which they lived, whether the school offered extended hours for the convenience of having their children supervised and safe while they were at work, and whether the school offered extracurricular activities that would engage their students and give them something to do that was productive after hours so that they stayed out of trouble (Kamenetz 2015).

Moreover, parents with low socioeconomic status cared even more than affluent parents about these other factors over academics. Taking all of these desires into account, it seems that what parents want most from their public schools is the village they have counted on that will help raise their child.

Educators' Desires

Of the groups of stakeholders who work most intimately in our schools, we also must include the desires of educators in our mission to uncover a more inspiring purpose for public education. Educators' desires are largely based on the belief systems that motivated them to go into teaching in the first place.

These belief systems are deeply ingrained into the psyche of most teachers, and they have a profound impact on their day-to-day decisions, behaviors, and interactions with others.

Each teacher can be categorized more or less by one of the following ideologies: social reconstructionism, academic rationalism, technologists, self-actualization, cognitive process, or religious orthodoxy. While many of these ideologies might be influencing a teacher at the same time, usually one is her dominant decision-driver (Costa & Garnston 2002).

Social reconstructionists believe that education's purpose is to improve society through the development of good citizens. These educators aim to instill in their students the values and skills that will allow them to someday become productive members of society who will ultimately improve the world in which we live. On the other end of the spectrum are those who are driven by the concept of self-actualization.

The view of those who believe in self-actualization is that the purpose of education is to honor the unique talents, abilities, and passion of each student in order to allow him to develop to his full potential. For those invested in self-actualization, the purpose of learning is solely for the benefit and development of the learner (Costa & Garnston 2002).

Academic rationalists believe that the adults in students' lives know what is best for them, and their job is to impart the wisdom they have gained in life to their students. On the other hand, those who identify with the cognitive process ideology believe that the purpose of schools is to develop the mind to its full capacity—to help students think more critically and problem solve effectively (Costa & Garnston 2002).

Technologists, however, tend to be driven by measurable gains. They consider the purpose of education to be providing students with measureable skills and knowledge similar to the way a business would produce a product. Accountability, test scores, using data to drive instruction, and student mastery is what drives their decisions. Finally, those driven by religious orthodoxy believe that the purpose of education is to teach the morals, values, and habits that are in accordance with how their religion tells them that people should live (Costa & Garnston 2002).

Even if educators largely lean toward a similar political position or stance on education policy, one cannot assume that educators are all driven by the same desired purpose for public education. This begs the question: if educators all have different purposes that influence their craft and drive their professional pursuits, are all of these belief systems mutually exclusive, or are some of them dependent upon each other and under the umbrella of an even larger purpose?

In other words, are these ideals really able to stand on their own, or, for example, does a social reconstructionist also need to invest in a student's passions, talents, and interests in order to inspire her someday to take an interest in the larger society and become a productive member of her community?

Regardless of their various ideologies, many educators in America today feel uninspired and demoralized by the current purpose of public education and the way the reformers carry out that purpose in schools. First of all, while a little over half of the country's teachers support the Common Core, the other half of educators say that they do not believe the Common Core will improve the quality of education in their communities, and thirty-four percent of teachers even said that they think it will have an adverse effect on students and the surrounding community (Schaffhauser 2015).

Imagine the struggle of these educators—regardless of whether their predications are correct—to remain inspired in their work when they believe that what they are being asked to do will have a negative impact on children. Education policies in America must be changed in order for teaching to become an attractive profession in which to work.

In most countries and circumstances where teachers fight for their rights, what they are fighting for is not better pay but better working conditions in schools. We might do well to listen to their desires, as international rankings of school systems show that in the places where teachers have more autonomy, better relationships with their superiors, and are respected by their communities, students' achievement is also better.

Being empowered by their leaders and their communities and being appreciated by society is not just a fluffy sentiment or wishful thinking by teachers. Teachers' effectiveness is directly related to the effectiveness of their leaders. Leaders who exhibit empathy and are attuned to others' moods literally affect the brain chemistry of their followers, which leads to inspired work and better outcomes.

Boyatziz and Goleman (2008) uncovered that social intelligence is the number one factor that inspires others to be effective. They found that leaders who had been hired for their work ethic, self-discipline, drive, and intelligence were sometimes fired for their lack of social intelligence. There is even a correlation between an organization's performance and how often the leader makes her subordinates laugh. High-performing leaders make their subordinates laugh three times as often as mid-performing leaders. What's more, being in a good mood, their research found, helps workers process information effectively and respond creatively and efficiently.

Is it possible that the narrative of failing schools in America and prevalence of lackluster teaching become a self-fulfilling prophecy? Legislators place pressure on educational leaders to come down on their subordinates with accountability measures and threats of rewards and sanctions, and then those leaders, in turn, pressure their teaching staff with those same threats and criticisms. Yet, the research clearly indicates that it is the culture of the school and the influence of the classroom teacher that will have the greatest impact on student outcome.

However, when people are under stress, adrenaline and cortisol have a major impact on their reasoning and cognition. While low levels of these hormones facilitate critical thinking and problem solving, when they are elevated by leaders' demands that seem insurmountable they can paralyze the mind's ability to function (Boyatzis & Goldman 2008). Seemingly, teachers, as well as students, need to be happy and hopeful in order to do their job well too. Maybe we should be putting as much effort into inspiring our teachers as we do in measuring their results.

Teachers may want different things for their students. Some may want to instill joy and passion. Some may want to empower their students to make the world a better place. Some wish to instill solid values and impart their wisdom on younger generations. All of these purposes, regardless of their differences, are noble, and likely are all interdependent as well.

If we can find a common ground—a purpose that speaks to all of the various belief systems that educators bring to the table—and if we can align our day-to-day practices with that common purpose, then educators will likely find inspiration in their work. They will have the drive to make the difference in students' lives and in their futures that we have tasked them with making.

If, however, we demonstrate with our words and actions that educators' purpose is to make their school, district, state, or country look good at the expense of the children actually doing and feeling good, they will never have the intrinsic drive that it takes to move the mountains of inequity and opportunity in public education in America. After all, taking into account educators' desires, we can infer that what they really want is to make a difference.

Simply making someone else look good is not making any real difference whatsoever. If our mission is to facilitate a sense of purpose that inspires stakeholders of public education in America, we need to, at the very least, make sure that our purpose is inspiring to those tasked with carrying it out.

Colleges' and Employers' Desires

If college and career readiness is truly to remain our mission in public education, then we would be wise to look at what university professors and employers desire from public education as well. One might assume that educators' and families' desires are contradictory to the aims of college and career readiness. But, actually, employers' and college professors' desires are more congruent with the desires of those in the trenches of the schools than we might guess.

The world's top employers are currently demanding a lot from their applicants. However, what they are demanding is much broader than simply a college degree. They are more interested, in fact, with applicants' soft skills. The world's top businesses want employees who can work together effectively, be flexible and adapt to changes, demonstrate humility and sensitivity to various cultures and viewpoints, and communicate clearly and effectively (Wiseman 2013).

Most employers do not fire their employees for lack of technical skill or knowledge but for issues like not being able to work well on a team or demonstrate a professional attitude and work ethic (Wiseman 2013). It makes sense then that a large desire of employers is for our public school system to instill these soft skills in their future employees. Basically, business leaders want public schools to create well-rounded workers and not simply technically competent and academically proficient workers.

Recent research gives validity to employers' desires. According to Achor (2011), only twenty-five percent of job success is determined by an employee's IQ or academic ability. Seventy-five percent, however, is determined by employees' optimism, social support, and ability to handle stress. In other words, an employee's emotional state is a much better indicator of his productivity and success in the company than his competence in the technical aspects of the work.

Unfortunately, in February 2015, only thirty-three percent of U.S. employees stated that they were engaged at their place of employment, and this percentage was the highest monthly average that has been recorded in over three years. The peak engagement level of American workers happened back in 2011 with a whopping thirty-four percent of employees saying that they were engaged at work (Adkins 2015). According to Adkins (2015), workplace engagement is the number one factor of future business success, affecting outcomes such as employee turnover, profitability, and productivity.

Not surprisingly as employee engagement increases, companies grow. And, as companies grow, the U.S. economy improves. What we want most, it seems, is engaged students because engaged students will someday become engaged citizens and workers. Public education, however, is founded on the idea (that dates back to the Industrial Revolution) that it is primarily intelligence, not engagement, which leads to success.

Our students, our teachers, our parents, and even our business leaders clearly do not buy this idea though—mostly because it hasn't worked. The more we have pushed the solely academic agenda, the more we have drained the passion, creativity, and intrinsic drive to learn out of our schools. Schools are told they are failing more than ever before in American history, and students are being diagnosed with attention disorders more than ever before in history.

We have an epidemic of ADHD in our country, and the diagnosis of this disorder has risen proportionately with the growth of standardized testing and the decline of the arts and other inherently engaging subjects in schools. The arts engage most students so much that they feel fully alive and in a peak state of flow. When students have the opportunity to use their creativity, their senses are operating at their highest capacity (Robinson 2008).

Yet, since we have narrowed the curriculum so much in order to focus on the core subjects at the expense of the arts and students' need for creativity, we resort to getting our students through the day by medicating them with drugs that are quite literally anesthetics—sedatives that shut off the same senses that would otherwise be awakened through an engaging curriculum (Robinson 2008).

This is not the desire though of our stakeholders whose voices should carry the most weight in the discussion on the purpose of public education. It is clear that families, educators, and employers alike want public education to produce passionate, happy, and inspired human beings who are ready to pursue their passions and contribute to society . . . and in doing so their unique interests and talents will propel them to work hard, innovate, and improve our world.

A *symptom* of this passion and inspiration will likely be that the United States of America becomes a beacon for economic equity and prosperity and a leader in the world in terms of national well-being because its individual citizens are well. It is somewhat ironic that Bill Gates, the man behind much of the recent reform in public education, is a college dropout. Clearly he is an intelligent man.

But, was it his college and career readiness that propelled him to his billionaire status and initiated his insatiable desire to make the world a better place? Was it his academic skills and knowledge that moved him to take on the larger-than-life goals of equity and opportunity in education and the promotion of global health and well-being? Or, was it his passion, desire for fulfillment, and sense of purpose that made him the influential man he is today?

Public school standards dictate what we focus on and prioritize in schools. These standards address both our society's civic and economic needs but largely ignore society's social needs. Because our social well-being impacts our economic and civic well-being, this is a colossal oversight on the part of educational leaders. It is the spirit of the American people and not their academic proficiency that has helped the United States to remain a global superpower.

In order to cultivate the spirit of American citizens we must first activate their internal drive as children. How far will knowledge and skill alone go if they aren't accompanied by passion and drive? Our emotional state and our soft skills are integral to our future success and happiness as individuals and as a society. Even if we have different aims for public education, that is, economic prosperity, national power, personal power, fulfillment, etc., it appears that the path to these various goals is the same: the activation of our internal drive.

Maybe this path—since it leads to all of our various destinations—*should* be the end goal of public education in America. This is the undercurrent of all stakeholders' desires. It is the intersection of all our hopes. Of course we need to foster high standards for academic achievement in schools. But academic achievement in school is a symptom of students' intrinsic drive and not the other way around.

If the general health of our public education system is failing, then we need to treat the cause and not the symptoms. Education is more than just the transmission of information. It is a tool for human growth and fulfillment. We need to use this tool to inspire our children. We need to give them hope—to fill their hearts and feed their spirits. This is the true purpose of education.

Chapter 5

Finding a Noble Purpose

A PURPOSE THAT INSPIRES

Current and past reforms in public education in America have been shortsighted. They do not and have not honored the complexities this organic and human industry brings to the table. We should not fault the intentions of those behind these reforms, but we should acknowledge that their shortsighted aims are uninspiring. College and career readiness, economic prosperity, civic responsibility, social status, and good health will be natural side effects of coming together around a nobler and more inspiring purpose: the internal drive of our students.

More important even than ensuring that our students learn is ensuring that our students *want* to learn. This internal drive is dependent upon their emotional well-being, their hope for the future, and their passion and engagement in their learning. And, no, we should not lower our expectations to focus on these things. In fact, once we begin to pursue these things, it is reasonable to expect that we could even raise our expectations of our students.

We have it backward. Instead of teaching and assessing with a laser-like focus only the academic content we want students to master in schools so they can become college and career ready, we should be assessing the soft skills and motivation students possess. We must do this to ensure that they can access the academic skills and knowledge and *care* enough about the skills and knowledge to do something productive, ethical, and fulfilling with them.

After all, there are plenty of concepts that we as adults understand and skills that we possess that we do not put into use simply because we do not have the intrinsic drive to do so. Application of knowledge and skill is dependent upon that drive. In fact, even if people are able to apply their knowledge and skill in spite of their lack of intrinsic drive, there are still ramifications for their well-being.

> Often, people are good at things they don't really care for. It's about passion and what excites our spirit and our energy. And if you're doing the thing you love to do, that you're good at, time takes a different course entirely. . . . You know this, if you're doing something you love, an hour feels like five minutes. If you're doing something that doesn't resonate with your spirit, five minutes feels like an hour. And the reason so many people are opting out of education is because it doesn't feed their spirit, it doesn't feed their energy or their passion (Robinson 2010, 13:48).

As a country, we spend more on public education than any other nation in the world. Yet, compared to other countries, we also have some of the lowest high-school graduation rates. Our problems in public education are complicated, and fixing them will require complex thinking and approaching the issues from multiple angles. Silver bullet reforms will not make an impact.

However, regardless of the complexity of the task, the only way it will be surmountable is if we approach it with a common understanding of what we are trying to accomplish—our true purpose in public education. This inspiring purpose will serve as a motivator for educators, parents, students, and the larger community. In order to understand how to address these complexities, it is important to look at the places where public education in America is working.

The educational programs that have been proven to work time and again are often found in "alternative schools" or schools that are designed to meet the needs of our students who fail to thrive in traditional settings. These programs work by tapping into students' individual interests and passions. They first help them realize what they are good at and then build on those skills and celebrate those strengths.

These programs work because they put the humanity back into the learning. They treat education like the multifaceted and personal process that it is and not the one-size-fits-all standardized process that it has become. These programs are successful because people who love what they do and are intrinsically driven are in their element—they are able to reach that peak state of flow that leads to achievement beyond what they thought was possible. According to Robinson (2013), we need to find a way for students and teachers to feel in their element.

But what then do we make of the national movement to increase our competencies in the areas of math and science in order to lead to innovations that will propel our nation to the top of the global economy? If it is true that there is such a need for engineers and innovators, don't we need to be content and standards oriented over student oriented? How can we foster the unique passions of individuals if we have specific needs as a country? It turns out that engineers, mathematicians, and scientists are not the only minds behind the innovation of companies that lead the global marketplace.

In Silicon Valley, ninety percent of CEOs and heads of product engineering have college degrees. Of those ninety percent, only four out of every ten have degrees in engineering or math. The rest have degrees in business, arts, or humanities. In fact, after college, only about a third of college graduates in general join careers that directly relate to their college degrees (Robinson 2013). In short, the innovators of Silicon Valley are not the ones with advanced knowledge in mathematics and science; they are the ones with advanced creativity and passion.

Surprisingly, or not so surprisingly, after seven years of research and 500 interviews later, success expert, Richard St. John (2005), identified what he believes are the key elements of success; and they are utterly synonymous with Robbins's (2006) theory of our six basic human needs, Dweck's (2006) theory of growth versus fixed mind-sets, Pink's (2011) theory of drive, Duckworth's (2013) theory on grit, and Robinson's (2006) theories on passion and creativity.

St. John pinpointed the secrets of success as *passion* (doing something for the love of the thing and not the money or accolades), *hard work and persistence* (grit), *being good at a thing* (mastery/significance), *focus* (part of grit—holding onto your dreams amidst challenges and setbacks), *pushing oneself* (personal growth and a growth mind-set), *serving others* (contribution/purpose), and *the possession of good ideas* (creativity). These traits not only lead to economic prosperity for society, but they impact our individual fulfillment as well as our civic and social growth.

So, how do we not only foster these things in schools but make them and the internal drive they create in students the central mission of our schools? If inspiring students to harness their passion and pursue their purpose was to become the central mission of schools (and academics were to simply become the vehicle used to carry it out), then schools and school systems would need to change in significant ways to reflect these greater priorities.

Similar to the backward design process the writers of the Common Core utilized to create the new national standards, we would need to start with where we would hope students would be in regards to their intrinsic drive by the time they graduated high school. If our primary purpose for public education is to ignite students' intrinsic drive so that they are motivated to go out into the world and contribute their talents for the greater good of society, then it would make sense that by the time students graduated they had both an awareness of their passions and the skills and knowledge necessary for them to pursue those passions.

OUT WITH REFORM AND IN WITH REVOLUTION

Reform is worthless in education because we cannot expect to make changes to a profoundly broken model of education that will result in ideal outcomes for students and society. What we can expect, however, is that revolutionizing the entire system of education might result in revolutionary changes in students and society. Innovation in education is difficult. It means starting with a blank slate, reexamining our true purpose, and systematically designing an entirely new system in which all components are geared toward realizing that purpose.

The first step in ensuring that our students leave high school with a solid understanding of their passions and an insatiable thirst for who they can become is to rethink social promotion and the current factory model of schools. The current education model, according to Robinson (2008), was created for the age of industrialization and created in the image of industrialization. There is a certain production-line mentality to grouping children by age and sending them to separate wings of separate buildings to learn separate subjects. Robinson challenges us to question the idea that the most important thing that children have in common is their age.

Presently in public education, students are promoted to each grade level on the basis of their age rather than on mastery of the content. As students progress in grades, the gap in students' abilities widens considerably as often does the gap in their hopefulness and engagement. If mastery is such an essential component to intrinsic drive, then we must find ways to foster mastery for all of our students. In fact, there may not be much reason any more for grade levels at all.

Rather than teachers being in charge of a certain grade level or certain subject area, what if they were in charge of clusters of standards? As students mastered those clusters of standards, they could move on to the next cluster that builds on the academic, social, and emotional knowledge and skills they just acquired. This would allow for students to grow at their own pace and move through developmental and cognitive stages as they are ready for them. This sense of mastery would enhance students' engagement and internal drive.

More than just moving students through school based on mastery of standards, though, we should also let their passions dictate their trajectory. In a moderate-sized school district there might be a handful of elementary schools, and in each of those schools there are often three or four teachers at each grade level. It seems that with so many schools and so many teachers within each school that different schools in the district could be based on varying students' interests, or mini schools within schools could honor children's varying passions.

For example, rather than attending a school based on geographical boundaries, why couldn't children choose a school that integrated the academic standards with art, music, athletics, engineering, or other topics in order to tap into students' passions? What's more, transition in and out of these schools or mini schools could be fluid based on students' changing interests. If student drive and engagement were our primary purposes, then keeping them engrossed in the learning would have to become our priority.

Robinson (2010) suggests that we get rid of linearity all together in public education and create a more organic system based on students' unique needs and talents. What would happen if time and age held less influence in our children's education, and instead they left school and went on to college and/or the workforce when they had developed the soft skills, social/emotional readiness, and academic prowess they needed in life in addition to the internal drive to do something with those skills?

> We have to go from what is essentially an industrial model of education, a manufacturing model, which is based on linearity and conformity and batching people and move to a model that is based more on principles of agriculture. We have to recognize that human flourishing is not a mechanical process; it's an organic process. And, you cannot predict the outcome of human development. All you can do, like a farmer, is create the conditions under which they will begin to flourish (Robinson 2010, 14:30).

If we are to broaden our understanding of how students could be grouped differently throughout their schooling, then we must also broaden our understanding of the skills and concepts worth learning. We must increase the options for students in terms of what they can learn in school, which would take on an entirely different approach than our current narrowing of the curriculum.

Presently, everything we do in education is about standardization and conformity. If we wish to ignite students' intrinsic drive and eventually produce citizens who have something of value to contribute to society, we need to move in the exact opposite direction: we need creativity (having original ideas of value) and divergent thinking (being able to approach a problem from several different angles) to serve as the backbone of our public school system—not standardization and conformity (Robinson 2008).

Instead, in our current system, students' ability to think creatively and divergently decreases over time as they "advance" in their education. The "paperclip test" is a study that illustrates this phenomenon. In the study, students were asked to brainstorm how many different ways they could think of to use a paperclip. The more ideas students came up with, the more creative and divergent they were considered to be.

In kindergarten, an astounding ninety-eight percent scored in the "genius level." This percentage, however, decreased exponentially each year students moved through school. Essentially, students became less creative the more "educated" they became (Robinson 2008). According to Robinson, this lack of creativity and divergent thinking in schools is leading to a human resources crisis as dire and as important to address as the climate crisis we are currently facing.

In order to address this human resource deficit, we need to broaden the curriculum by bringing back the subjects that wake up our students' senses and that put the joy at the center of their learning. Art, music, physical education, drama, etc., are not extras. They are not luxuries that should be saved only for the students who have mastered the prerequisites. They should be the lenses through which we learn other disciplines.

Moreover, science, math, language arts, and social studies are not compartmentalized in life the way we compartmentalize them in school. In life and in our places of work we do not set aside an hour chunk of our day for writing, an hour to read, another time to problem solve, and yet another to catch up on the current events in our world or in our industry. So, why do we do this in school? We must make students' learning relevant to their lives.

One way to ignite students' interest and make the learning relevant to their lives is to rethink the design of learning standards. Currently, the standards are issued as a giant laundry list of learning skills and concepts that students are expected to master at each grade level. Because the list of standards is inevitably too cumbersome to teach with any depth over the course of a year, some districts and states prioritize the standards and put more emphasis and focus on the priority standards than the others.

When prioritizing standards, districts and states may look at standards that are the most important for college and career readiness and commit to teaching those standards more in-depth and assessing those standards explicitly and frequently in classrooms. What is strange is that standards are listed as a series of independent learning goals. While they may be listed under an overarching heading, such as "informational reading," the informational reading standards that follow are still simply listed one by one.

What is odd about this is that the learning of those concepts and skills does not happen in that linear or isolated fashion. Many of the standards are interdependent, and arguably even as a cluster of interrelated skills and concepts, they do not reflect the most essential skills and knowledge that students need.

For example, many grades in states that have adopted the Common Core Standards have language arts standards that talk about citing text evidence to support one's analysis of the text, writing arguments to support one's claims, and having collaborative discussions where one listens to others' ideas and expresses his/her own clearly. These are just a few examples of some language arts standards, but it is clear how they might be interrelated.

The gist, when we look at these standards as an interrelated group, is that we want students to become adults who can express their own opinions effectively while respecting others in the conversation and keeping an open mind to their points of view. If students could leave school with this skill set, our society would surely be a better place. Teachers and curriculum writers who fail to see this larger goal of providing students with the skills of expression and collaboration and attempt to teach the standards in a checklist fashion rather than holistically, will fail to keep the purpose of the standards—the reason they were likely written in the first place—at the forefront of their instruction.

However, having a priority cluster of standards alone is not what sparks most students' intrinsic drive. The beauty of the standards is that the lens or content through which the standards are taught is not determined by the federal government, the states, or often not even by districts. One way to maintain the rigor of the standards while simultaneously activating our students' passion and motivation is to cluster standards at each grade level under concepts and skills that are not only essential for college and career readiness but are also simply essential to being human.

We have examined the importance of soft skills in life and in the context of college and career readiness. We have also discussed the idea that happiness leads to success and not the other way around. For these reasons, it would be wise to create supreme standards—standards that overarch both the priority and supporting standards and thus become the primary emphasis of our instruction and our assessment.

These supreme standards should take into account students' social and emotional development and the social and emotional skills and knowledge—the soft skills—that will lead to the most opportunity for happiness and success both now and in the future. This is especially important and especially doable if we maintain social promotion in schools and continue to assume that age is the most important characteristic shared by students.

Take middle school students, for example. What is most important to students at this stage is their social status. This is a time of much confusion for many pubescent and prepubescent preteens. Their hormones and emotions are all over the place; many are insecure; and their primary goal in life and in school is searching for acceptance from their peers. And yet, nowhere in the standards do we address this need for autonomy and significance even though this is the stage where these human needs are screaming to be fulfilled.

Instead, we might frame the learning and the standards only in issues and texts that seem irrelevant to students. As much as content like ancient Greece or astronomy might be important to understand, social competency is equally important. What if we created a supreme standard for students in this stage of development that overarched the academic standards? What if the supreme standard were something like, "Students will understand and apply healthy strategies for interacting with their peers."

Or another one could be, "Students will find ways to exert their autonomy that foster trust from others and promote confidence in their own abilities and decisions." What if standards like these were the main aim of the instruction, and the academic standards were used to support this purpose? Would students be more or less prepared for college and career? Would they be more or less engaged . . . more or less hopeful? Would we be contributing to their well-being or sweeping it under the rug?

Moreover, it wouldn't be too difficult to foster rigor while focusing on relevance. Imagine the richness of students' discussions and argumentative essays if the texts they used and the content they were studying were relevant to their lives in this way? Imagine what we could find out about students and how we could support them on their journey through school if our assessments were based on these supreme standards *as well as* the priority academic standards?

Through the use of student surveys and anecdotal data collected through observation, we could assess students' abilities to exert their autonomy responsibly. What's more, if we found that students were struggling in this area, we could intervene before it was too late—before they found unhealthy ways to have their needs of significance and belonging met. I propose that we keep the Common Core but use it to ignite and assess the *student's* core.

So, what would this look like for math? According to Wolfram (2010), one of our largest problems in math instruction in this country is that no one is very happy with it. Teachers complain that they do not have the skills or resources to teach it well, and students complain that the content is irrelevant to their lives and either too difficult and abstract or too boring. Wolfram states that this is a huge problem because math competency is such a mammoth requirement for our economic health as a country right now.

Part of the reason for the disconnection he says is because our math instruction in schools does not reflect real-world math whatsoever. Real-world math is more relevant to regular careers—engineers, biologists, geologists, and other regular professionals—than we recognize by our math instruction in schools. Based on our math instruction in schools, one would think that math is only done by mathematicians.

Wolfram (2010) argues that math is still an important compulsory subject in public education, but maybe it's time to give math a new name or umbrella it under more relevant topics. The reason for the new name or the new spin on math is that the entire subject of math has changed in recent years. Often people associate mathematics with computation. However, computation is unnecessary in this day and age; and we shouldn't be wasting our time in schools teaching children how to complete longhand algorithms.

The importance of math lies in the concepts and problem-solving skills that students gain through grappling with real-world questions, such as which is the best insurance policy to get; what is the best cell phone plan to buy; or what is the most profitable avenue for investing in retirement? Moreover, Wolfram (2010) reasons that it's time to take calculating out of the equation entirely in schools. With the advancement of technology, calculating is becoming irrelevant and unimportant. In the real world, computers calculate for us.

Students know this, and because of this knowledge not only do they get frustrated with the "drill-and-kill" monotony of calculating throughout their schooling, but the students who need to be most engaged—our students from poverty—often receive the most "drill-and-kill" instruction in an attempt to help them master the basics. The basics, however, are not even necessary to master anymore, argues Wolfram (2010).

He uses the analogy of how a hundred years ago it was necessary to understand the basics of motor vehicles because if you didn't you could not successfully operate them. However, with the current automation of cars, one doesn't need to know the basics of how all the parts work and work together. One must only know how to operate the car. The same is true, he states, for math.

We are wasting precious time helping students master the basics and teaching them how to calculate. What we should be doing, he says, is using math instruction to prepare them to become innovators, to prepare them for real life in whatever professional endeavor they pursue and to exercise their minds so that they train their brains for logical thinking and complex problem solving. Math is a set of skills and concepts to be applied in real-world settings. It is useful in many professions and is applicable to many topics. Maybe we should not make the end goal the understanding of math but rather the application of math in order to get better at these real-world professions and pursuits.

In fact, some places are experimenting with getting rid of subjects altogether in school. Instead of compartmentalizing the learning by discipline, that is, math, reading, writing, science, social studies, music, etc., countries like Finland are deciding to group the learning by topic, as learning by topic is a better reflection of the learning we do in the real world.

By 2020, Finland plans to do away with students enrolling in individual subjects and instead teach students under the umbrella of broader topics and phenomena so that students no longer feel the need to question teachers about the point and purpose of the learning. The point and the purpose of the learning becomes the course itself (MacDonald 2015).

What might this look like? Instead of spending an hour in math class, and then transitioning into language arts, and then to civics, a student might spend two or three hours in applied nutrition where they use math, communication, and civic responsibly as methods to understand and apply real-world professional and/or personal pursuits in the field of nutrition.

Because we have access to sophisticated technology in advanced industrialized countries, there is no reason we should spend the bulk of our time in school memorizing facts and figures. Rather, we should spend our time learning how to apply the information that we have access to at the tips of our fingers. What would be even more inspiring to students and relevant to their learning is the ability to apply these skills and knowledge in real time in real communities to make them better places to live.

Since the phasing out of individual subjects began in 2013, Finland has seen improvement in student outcomes. However, this shift hasn't been easy for Finland's teachers who have spent the majority of their careers specializing in isolated subjects. Policymakers must provide time and money for teachers to work together to create such engaging and relevant topics and to develop curricula that aims to integrate various subjects into them.

However, it is not enough to simply rethink our math standards and curriculum; we must rethink math assessment as well. How do we focus on and foster the soft skills in math the same way that we do in subjects where language arts standards are integrated? Is math ability and math achievement the prominent factors in innovators' success or is it something else? What if we spent as much time assessing students' soft skills and motivation in math as we do assessing their abilities?

What if we analyzed and provided feedback on qualities such as perseverance, curiosity, precision, collaboration, and the ability to tackle problems from multiple angles? What is more essential for innovation and problem solving later in life: skill or determination? Arguably they both are necessary, but currently we focus primarily on skill.

ASSESSMENT AND ACCOUNTABILITY

Assessment and accountability, in general, need rethinking. There is certainly a place for standardized assessment. It is important to gather information about our students' learning in schools. It is also important that we evaluate teachers and hold them to high standards of professionalism and growth. However, in doing so, it is also necessary that the data and information we collect are multidimensional so that we get a full picture of the learning and growth happening in schools—one that captures the complexities of such an organic and individualized endeavor.

One way to do this, according to the Bill and Melinda Gates Foundation (2013), is through the administration of student perception surveys.

> No one has a bigger stake in teaching effectiveness than students. Nor are there any better experts on how teaching is experienced by its intended beneficiaries. But only recently have many policymakers and practitioners come to recognize that—when asked the right questions, in the right ways—students can be an important source of information on the quality of teaching and the learning environment of individual classrooms (Retrieved from http://www.newtechnetwork.org/sites/default/files/resources/2014ntnstudentoutcomesreport1.pdf).

Student perception surveys are more reliable than some may believe. Asking students to answer specific questions that reflect the quality of their teachers' instruction is actually a more reliable measure than measures of student achievement gains and supervisor observations of instruction. One of the reasons that this may be is that students' perceptions reflect hours upon hours of time in the classroom spent being the recipient of teachers' instruction, whereas supervisor observations only capture a small snapshot of teaching over the course of a year.

Additionally, supervisor observations often only address the perceived quality of instruction and not the actual learning of students. Another reason that student perception surveys are often superior evaluation tools to observation and standardized assessment measures is because student surveys can actually provide more specific feedback to teachers on where they can improve.

The implementation of student surveys is as important as the surveys themselves. It is crucial that we measure what matters most, that we ensure accuracy and reliability, and that the results are used to support teacher improvement. The Bill and Melinda Gates Foundation (2013) suggests that we measure the following components of teacher instruction and classroom environment: care, control, clarify, challenge, captivate, confer, and consolidate.

The Gates Foundation (2013) suggests asking students about the level of care their teacher demonstrates by agreeing or disagreeing with statements such as "My teacher recognizes when something is bothering me." Their responses to this statement also reflect the degree to which their teacher fosters and is concerned about their well-being and the degree to which they feel connection to their teacher. This well-being and connection are prerequisites to the activation of their internal drive.

Survey items about teachers' control of the class include statements like "My classmates behave according to my teacher's expectations." Their responses to statements like these indicate the level of safety and expectations the teacher fosters in his classroom. Agreeing with statements such as this one indicates that the students' need for certainty is met by the teacher and by the classroom environment. Again, this certainty contributes to the students' overall well-being and engagement, and the fulfillment of these needs is also necessary if our hope is to have intrinsically motivated learners.

Teachers must also know when and how to clarify students' understanding and when and how to challenge students in class. Statements such as "My teacher is able to tell when our class understands the material and when we don't," and "In this class, the teacher helps us correct our mistakes," illustrate the degree to which the teacher fosters mastery in his instruction. Challenge also sparks excitement in the learning—fulfilling the students' need for uncertainty. This mastery of the content and skills and uncertainty in the learning are other factors that contribute to students' internal drive.

In addition, teachers' ability to captivate their students with instruction is a contributor to students' drive in school. Agreeing with survey items such as "The learning we do in here is interesting and enjoyable" reflects how much the students feel that the teacher nurtures their interests and passions in class. If students indicate with survey items that their teacher wants them to share their thoughts and feelings, then what they are really indicating is that their autonomy and significance are being cultivated. This autonomy and significance, as we have examined already, is integral for activating students' drive.

The final area to assess on student perception surveys, according to the Gates Foundation (2013), is teachers' ability to consolidate—to give feedback to students that leads to their growth and improvement. If students suggest that their teacher is strong in this area, what they are saying is that their need for growth is being met, as their teacher knows how to help them continue to improve as learners and as people. Growth is a fundamental need of all human beings, and if students aren't growing then they are not going to be fulfilled, and their internal drive is not going to be activated.

We would do well to offer two more "C's" to the items on the Gates student survey: contribution and commitment. With statements like "What I have to offer in this class is important and beneficial to others" and "The learning we do here is meaningful, and I feel committed to learning it" we would understand the degree to which teachers promote contribution and a sense of purpose in their classrooms, as contribution and a sense of purpose are essential to student motivation.

If we do design a better system of teacher evaluation that provides more accurate information about teachers' quality of instruction, how do we then improve, reward, and replicate quality teaching? Goodall (2015) suggests that we look at what successful companies do for ideas. In successful companies, yearly goals and annual evaluations do nothing to improve the quality of work by employees. Goal setting and evaluation, rather, happens frequently with supervisors evaluating the completion of many projects over the course of a year.

This idea could be used in education, as well. Rather than trying to paint a picture of effectiveness by looking at the growth of students over the course of a year with standardized test results and doing a few observations a year to gauge the quality of the teacher's instruction, what if principals met prior to certain units and standards being taught to set goals with educators and then checked in frequently through the course of that unit to support and evaluate the instruction?

The more data we can collect about our effectiveness with students the more likely we are to know exactly where to grow professionally and how to go about doing it. Enlisting the feedback of students and supervisors will help to paint a more detailed picture of our work, but enlisting the feedback of our peers will help to complete that picture. Many of us spend the majority of our careers operating as independent contractors within the school building. We only see our rung of the ladder of student growth and we miss out on the amazing benefits of collaborating with our colleagues in order to improve student achievement.

In Japan, many schools are working to utilize peer collaboration and observation as a means of improving instruction and student outcome. Japanese lesson study is a recent initiative in which teachers collaborate often to goal-set and plan with an extreme focus on the science of effective lesson planning. Teachers then take turns teaching the lesson and observing each other in order to analyze its effectiveness.

Then they meet for a post-lesson discussion to collaborate about what they have learned and use their new understandings to inspire future lesson design. Teachers in Japan have experienced much success with this model, and some even say that it is the most impactful professional development we can employ in our schools.

The structure of our education system does not just need to change for the betterment of our students. We need to change it to maximize educators' potential as well. We need to ensure that we are kindling teachers' will-drivers as well as their passion and well-being, as these things are essential to the classroom environment and quality of instruction. We need to ensure that teachers can achieve a sense of mastery by not setting them up for failure with a curriculum that is irrelevant to students and standards that are unattainable for some.

We cannot put a student who is operating at a second-grade level in a fourth-gade classroom simply because he is nine and then humiliate and berate the teacher when she cannot get him to grow three grade levels in one year. We also cannot hand teachers scripted, "teacher-proof" curricula, tell them that they have to follow it with fidelity, strip them of their creativity and autonomy, and then expect them to teach with passion and differentiate for the various interests of each student.

Finally, we cannot continue to simply tell educators what to do and how to do it while ignoring why we are asking them to do these things in the first place. As Sinek (2009) states, leaders are those who are in a position of power over others. Those who lead, however, are the ones who inspire us regardless of their position. We have to ensure that our purpose in doing what we do in public education is ethical and inspiring. Then we must ensure that it is transparent so that those in the trenches can continue to be inspired by its steadfast presence.

There are only two ways to influence people. You can influence them by manipulating them, or you can influence them by inspiring them (Sinek 2009). Let's stop manipulating our educators. Let's inspire them with a purpose that reignites their passion and reminds them of the reasons they entered this profession in the first place. Let's adopt a nobler purpose for education—one that is actually for the benefit of our children.

Inspiring our teachers and students does not mean that we have to lower our expectations or hold them less accountable. As mentioned previously, inspired people will give their blood, sweat, and tears to their mission. When our teachers and students put their blood, sweat, and tears into their work, we should expect them to achieve beyond our wildest dreams. With inspiration as the foundation of our teaching and learning, we will not need to use manipulation—rewards and sanctions for standardized testing results—to invoke fear in our educators.

Instead, standardized testing outcomes could be seen as the symptom of inspired learning that they are meant to be, not the end goal that they have become. Assessments and accountability are not inherently evil. However, when we neglect to start with the *why*—to lead with our purpose—we can easily lose sight of our mission and think that the measure is the prize to be won. The assessment results are not the prize; the prize is inspired American citizens operating at their full potential.

CREATING THE VILLAGE

We cannot simply change the structure of our schools, the content of our curriculum, and the methods of our assessment, however. We must also change the mind-set of the public so that the ethos of our communities and the culture of American society is that which supports public education and public educators. In the countries where students are performing at the top of the global pack, their citizens also hold teachers in high regard.

They understand that public education is the key to the future prosperity and well-being of their nations, and as such, they understand that teaching is one of the most valuable professions on the planet. Thus, they honor their teachers with optimal working conditions, high expectations for professionalism, and salaries that reflect the gravity of that with which they are tasked.

Real change in education and real change in society will take more than just supporting educators, though. Community entities need to partner together to surround students and their families with support and encouragement. Parents, businesses, doctors, social workers, and law enforcement officials need to become the village that it takes to raise these children and set into motion real opportunities for social mobility.

At this point in U.S. history, Americans are more segregated by class than ever before (Putnam 2015). The cultures of rich children and poor children are further apart than ever before. Even within the same town, the worlds of rich and poor children are entirely different. We are less likely than ever before in history to integrate by class in our geography, our social circles, schools, and our recreational activities.

Because of this separation, says Putnam (2015), we are heading toward a caste society. If we want to change this trajectory, we must realize that they are all "our kids" and take action to nurture them accordingly. Instead, the meaning of "our kids" has narrowed over time to quite literally mean my own biological kids. In essence, we've lost our village mentality when it comes to raising children in America.

People like the University of Florida's Nancy Hardt and Alachua County sheriff, Sadie Darnell, are attempting to right this wrong. This unlikely partnership began when Hardt, a pathologist in Gainesville, Florida, made it her mission to intervene in the lives of the most vulnerable children in her community. She knew that the research clearly showed that children who experience poverty, abuse, or neglect are more likely to become unhealthy adults and have shorter life spans than children who do not experience these traumas, and she wanted to change this trajectory for these children and for her community (Starecheski 2015).

Therefore, she looked at Medicaid records to analyze whether or not there were patterns in where Gainesville children were born into poverty. She found hotspots of extreme poverty in places that were sometimes surprising. Not knowing exactly what to do with this information, she took it to Sadie Darnell, the city's sheriff at the time.

Surprisingly, Darnell had created a similar map of her own: a thermal map of high crime incidents. Laying one map on top of the other, what they discovered was an exact match in location—a square-mile area—of high poverty and high crime. They knew instantly that the key to the community's well-being was doing something to improve the lives of those living in this square mile.

Their first step was to drive to that part of town and record their observations of all the things that made it hard for children to grow up healthy. Their list included things like poorly maintained subsidized housing, hunger, and a total lack of services, including medical care. In fact, they realized that the closest resource for medical care, the county health department, was almost a two-hour trip by bus each way.

Hardt instantly began to brainstorm ways she could address these issues. She went to work fundraising so that she could eventually purchase a large school bus with two exam rooms inside. Then she enlisted a considerable crew of volunteer doctors and medical students and raised money to hire a full-time driver and nurse for the mobile facility.

She parked her bus right outside the apartment complex at the center of the square-mile crime and poverty-ridden neighborhood and allowed patients to walk in without an appointment and receive care free of charge. The clinic was a success. Currently, 5,000 patients a year visit her mobile clinic. But the clinic, she admits, is just one piece of the puzzle when it comes to organizing a village to take care of our children.

Partnering with more local groups and grassroots organizers, Hardt eventually opened a family resource center right in the apartment complex where children could play supervised all day long. In addition, the organizers of the center offered free meals, computer access, Alcoholics Anonymous (AA) meetings, and now a permanent health clinic. All of the resources they developed were designed to decrease the likelihood of abuse and neglect by decreasing the ramifications of extreme poverty on families. They were essentially strengthening the most vulnerable families of their community. They were giving hope to an otherwise hopeless situation.

While common sense tells us that there is a correlation between poverty, health issues, and crime, seeing that connection quite literally on a map inspired Hardt and Darnell to do something about it, and since they took initiative to do something about this situation in their community, there has been a drop in the numbers of calls about child abuse and domestic violence. They admit they still have a long way to go in order to make a serious impact on the children's lives and their trajectory in society, but they know they will get nowhere by standing idly by while kids' lives are at stake (Starecheski 2015).

Since beginning this mission to improve the lives of children in poverty in her community, Hardt has realized that it is essential to partner with superintendents, principals, and teachers to identify which students in the community are struggling and how to help those students. The well-being of our children is a big deal. It is not a task that we can simply pawn off on educators while we go about our own business and hope that they have the tools, resources, and abilities to do the monumental work of changing lives. It is a job that we all must share if we truly want it done and want it done well.

It is not enough for community services to partner with schools. We need to bring parents into the equation too. Parents' socioeconomic status has a monumental influence on their child's success and well-being. And it's not simply the lack of money or resources that impacts their child's development; the level of toxic stress and the lack of positive parenting skills also have a profound influence. Poverty affects children's health and nutrition, vocabulary, effort and energy, mind-set, cognitive capacity, relationships, and stress level (Jensen 2013).

Children who grow up in low-income homes are more likely to be born premature or with disabilities and are less likely to exercise and eat nutritiously. In addition, children in poverty often have severely underdeveloped vocabularies. One study found that mothers from low-income families use fewer words when talking to their children than toddlers of middle- and high-income families use when talking to their parents (Bracey 2006). This is especially concerning considering that variation in students' vocabulary is one of the primary reasons for the achievement gap in schools (Jensen 2013).

Poverty affects students' mind-sets as well. Low socioeconomic status often correlates with a sense of helplessness in the present and hopelessness for the future (Rob, Simon, & Wardle 2009). This is problematic given that a student's mind-set in school is a strong predictor of her academic achievement. Sadly, low socioeconomic status is also associated with measures of low cognitive capacity on IQ and other achievement tests because poverty has a direct effect on the physical brain.

The hippocampus—a part of the brain responsible for new learning and memory—is smaller and has less volume in children from poverty (Amat et al. 2008; Hanson et al. 2011). It isn't hard to see how this will adversely affect impoverished children in school and how eventually the academic struggle they feel day in and day out reinforces their sense of helplessness and hopelessness.

Additionally, children who grow up in poverty often struggle to form and maintain healthy relationships. Children in poverty are more likely to be raised by a single parent (Bishaw & Renwick 2009), are less likely to learn appropriate emotional responses to everyday situations due to the lack of modeling from their overstressed caregivers (Malatesta & Izard 1984), and are less likely to receive positive and nurturing caregiving.

In fact, students from poor homes typically receive one positive affirmation to every two negative reprimands, whereas children from higher-income homes receive six positive affirmations to every one negative reprimand

(Hart & Risley 1995). The difference in positivity and worth students from poor and affluent families feel impacts the effort and energy they put forth in school and in life.

Finally, children from poverty experience much higher levels of stress than students from more affluent families. They experience more abuse, more overcrowding in their homes, more disruption of the family structure due to separations and dissolution of relationships, and harsher discipline often including physical punishment (Emery & Laumann-Billings 1998; Gershoff 2002; Lichter 1997; Slack et al. 2004). This chronic and acute stress often results in children responding with learned helplessness in as early as first grade.

The more stress and early trauma they encounter, the more likely they are to give up on life at an early age (Henry 2005). Yet, our current practice in many schools is to ignore all of these issues. We ignore them because we tell ourselves these things are out of our control. We also ignore them because addressing them seems insurmountable. We have no idea what to do or where to start, and even talking about parents' skills or lack thereof has become a taboo subject.

We don't want to hurt anyone's feelings by coming across as superior or condescending, and we are told that it is not alright to project our ideals and values onto others. Moreover, there are so many prevailing narratives about the culture of poverty in America—many that contradict each other, blame the victim, and aim to suppress the very culture that needs our help—that we stay clear of such a politically sensitive topic.

We owe it to our children to stop being cowards when it comes to this issue. We owe it to our children to stop dismissing their suffering. We can have a conversation about these issues and seek to develop solutions for addressing them without spending our time judging and placing blame.

If children need proper health care, access to the language of the prosperous, healthy models for positive responses to emotion and positive relationships, and parents who have the tools and strategies to foster a home environment conducive to proper development, then we must work to give this to them. Period. We can no longer avoid this issue while claiming to want what is best for kids.

One way to begin to tackle the family issues that correlate with poverty is to educate and empower parents. Schools need to become central hubs where stakeholders invested in the well-being of the community's children come together to build each other up and support each other so that they can then better support the children. It is time for Parent Teacher Associations (PTAs) to shift from primarily fundraising organizations to organizations whose aim it is to provide adults with tools and strategies to better grow these little human beings—organizations that provide teachers, parents, and community members with a platform in which they can work together to address students' needs.

Imagine the impact we could make if teachers and parents together examined the research around the environments and conditions most conducive to students' success and well-being and then worked to foster those environments. Imagine the social and emotional growth of our communities if stakeholders committed to each other to employ strategies and solutions that would improve the conditions under which children thrived. Imagine the increase in attendance at these meetings if they offered real hope for families and did not just ask them to raise funds for the school when they are already struggling to even raise funds for their child's next meal.

In order to inspire the stakeholders in the trenches of the work—our students, their parents, and our educators—we MUST actually operate in schools under a framework of what is best for kids and not under a framework of what will make us look better or will help us to receive more funding. We cannot simply say that our purpose is to activate students' internal drive and provide them with the skills and knowledge to utilize that drive. We must also believe it and use that belief to guide all of our actions.

If we have ulterior motives—if we say we want students to be inspired but what we really want is a data point that beats the competition—then our actions will not be congruent with our purpose and we will never realize the full potential of public education. We must come together around an inspiring purpose and then design everything we do under the umbrella of that mission. We must keep the *why* at the center of our work, day in and day out.

There are two fundamental components of the teaching and learning we do in schools—*what* we teach and *how* we teach it. The curriculum is the *what* and the instruction is the *how*. If our primary purpose is activating the internal drive of our students then we need to use our curriculum and instruction to do so. We need to make sure that what we teach and how we teach are aimed at making our students engaged, hopeful, and happy.

IMPLICATIONS FOR THE CURRICULUM

A quality curriculum is arguably a cornerstone of teaching and learning and has important benefits to educational institutions. An excellence curriculum can have a significant impact on student achievement. What's more, curriculum can be used as a tool for increased transparency and congruency in educational organizations.

When all stakeholders in the institution are aware of a clear and coherent curriculum, students are more reflective of their learning; staff understand better their role in helping achieve the desired outcome; teachers are more likely to collaborate; and administrators and members of the public are more likely to be in the know about the learning and expectations within the organization.

Curriculum often mirrors how humans think and is an attempt at combining and ordering ideas so that they can be learned deeply and efficiently. Naturally, since people often think differently from one another, different curricular theories in education have emerged. These theories include sequential curricula, which suggests a linear process of learning; spiral curricula, or a repeating presentation and practice of concepts and skills; thematic curricula, a collection of concepts under the umbrella of one topic of study; and integrated curricula, which brings together interdependent concepts and ideas in a holistic curricular format.

If curriculum is a major part of the equation in student learning, and there are so many differing curricular philosophies in practice, how does one know what is best to teach? At the foundation of students' ability to construct enduring understandings is curriculum design. Yet, many students fail to develop a sufficient understanding of key concepts because the instruction is based on a curriculum that is derived from textbooks, worksheets, or other activities that are not relevant or meaningful to students (Childre, Pope, & Sands 2009).

If we are to make activation of students' internal drive the purpose of public education, we should teach what is most meaningful and relevant to students. Chandler (2006) suggests that curriculum that connects to students' lives leads to greater achievement and depth of knowledge than traditional, departmentalized instruction. He states that when students are able to make curricular connections, they become more flexible thinkers and their work begins to exhibit multiple perspectives. Most importantly, when students feel a connection to what they are learning, they are more motivated and engaged in the learning.

Relevance, however, does not just imply student centeredness. A meaningful curriculum is one that creates connections between concepts and disciplines and reflects the interconnectedness, multidimensionality, and complexity of the real world. Curriculum should be designed around essential questions and a set of concepts to be explored, rather than around isolated subject areas such as social studies, reading, writing, math, and science.

For example, a teacher might pose the essential question, *Why is invention essential to society?* Under the umbrella of this guiding question a teacher may bring in history, reading, writing, and science to explore the big ideas that connect to this question. Therefore, these subject areas are all learned through a lens that has relevance to the students in that this broad, overarching perspective provides them with enduring understandings about the world as well as connections between those understandings and the foundational skills they are developing in each subject area.

A relevant curriculum, though, is not limited to connecting studies to students' preexisting interests; rather a relevant curriculum is one that is challenging to students and creates new interests. When the curriculum is meaningful and is grounded in wonder, students become more invested in the learning and find the content to be more meaningful to their lives. Teachers, too, are motivated by relevance. When teachers take part in the design of a meaningful and relevant curriculum, they are inspired to make pedagogical and structural changes to their lessons that improve student learning (Murata 2002).

Because there are so many subjects and standards that teachers are required to teach and because there is not enough time in the year to teach these standards, it can be argued that developing an integrated curriculum is necessary. However, an integrated curriculum is not only a more efficient way to address the numerous concepts and skills that students must know and be able to do; an integrated curriculum can create a deeper emotional connection between the students and the subject areas, a greater understanding of the concepts being taught, more motivation for learning, and greater self-efficacy among students.

Furthermore, a holistic and integrated curriculum has not only been shown to provide more relevance for students but is also argued to be more rigorous because it is more complex than a traditional curriculum. One reason for this is that often in an integrated curriculum the students learn through inquiry as opposed to the teacher simply distributing the knowledge to the students. Because subjects are interconnected and reflect real-world understanding, real-world problem solving is often required. This discovery model that is founded in problem solving demands that the students think critically.

Although the pendulum of curriculum theory over the course of American history has swung back and forth from student centeredness to traditionalism (founded in the basic concepts and skills that students must know and be able to do), many current researchers argue that the most effective curriculum provides a balance of both theories. For, a curriculum that is relevant to students must be one that illustrates the connectedness and complexity of life. A truly relevant curriculum is, by nature, rigorous.

Additionally, it is true that critical thinking is necessary in preparing students to succeed in postsecondary education as well as in a complex and ever-increasing intellectually sophisticated society. Students should be prepared to make rational decisions and demonstrate sound judgment as citizens of an educated society, and to this end, the curriculum model in schools is of the utmost importance.

Likewise, the most rigorous curriculum is one that grounds essential skills in real-world controversy, as this type of curriculum is designed to nurture civic engagement and promote student voice. Critical thinking centered on issues that are relevant to students and society at large helps students develop their own ideas and beliefs, which, in turn, helps to foster democratic citizens who can evaluate ideas and take an educated stance on issues that impact the world.

Student centeredness and rigorous standards are not paradoxical but rather complimentary, and low-income schools with high populations of minority students have shown significant improvement in student achievement when delivering this kind of rigorous curriculum (Ferrero 2006). When students are asked to think critically, they perform better academically. Lesley (2001) found that students in remedial programs that focused on critical thinking outperformed their peers who were in similar programs that emphasized basic skills and knowledge.

Thus, a rigorous curriculum is not founded in memorization and mastery of the basics as a prerequisite to critical thinking. Rather, researchers suggest that a rigorous curriculum *begins* with a ploy to hook students on a problem or issue that requires critical thinking which in turn increases student motivation to master the basics. Students are motivated by challenge, and when students are challenged they will work much harder to become proficient in basic skills and master their academic goals.

Another component of a rigorous curriculum is the development of essential questions and big ideas. Open-ended questions that focus on the enduring understandings that have the most leverage for students' understanding of the world around them are instrumental in promoting student engagement as well as critical thinking (Lam, Radhakrishnan, & Schimmade 2011).

One approach to incorporate essential questions into curriculum design is the backward design model. Curriculum design is most effective when teachers start with the end in mind. By grouping like standards and creating big ideas and essential questions that get to the heart of why those standards are important for students to master, teachers can improve learning in their classrooms.

As a result of this backward design, the learning becomes deeper and these powerful, enduring questions beg students to continuously tap into their higher order thinking skills. By framing the learning with big ideas and essential questions, the concepts and skills also become more relevant to students.

Texts and resources that promote authentic literacy are also important to a rigorous curriculum. Authentic literacy involves reading, writing, and discussion about ideas central to a text and to the real world. When students are given the opportunity to critically analyze text, evaluate its merit, synthesize the information or ideas to form an opinion, and justify their reasoning with evidence, they are honing the skills that will help them become engaged and influential citizens in a democratic society.

A rigorous curriculum not only increases student learning but also, in turn, has the potential to positively impact society. Our duty as educators is to prepare students to become critical and analytical thinkers so that they can be successful in their personal and professional lives.

Many curricula in American schools are adopted by districts and mandated to teachers to execute in their classrooms. Not only are these curricula not always directly tied to the most essential learning and enduring understandings but often educators interpret and carry out the curricula differently. When the curriculum is carried out incompletely or incorrectly, teaching and learning can suffer. Deep implementation of the curriculum is crucial to student success. Reeves's (2010) work even indicates that half-hearted implementation of the curriculum is actually worse for students' understanding and achievement than no implementation at all.

In addition, teachers often show resistance to implementing mandated curricula or curriculum reform. In contrast, schools that demonstrate characteristics of ownership of and experimentation with the curriculum have been shown to have greater implementation of the curriculum and thus a greater impact on learning (Lam 2011). This could be because ownership of the curriculum fosters teacher autonomy.

Teachers who are allowed to develop their own curriculum or experiment with the curriculum that has been provided to them are more likely to view themselves as learners and are more reflective in their practice (Petrie 2012). Therefore, we should advocate for a grassroots approach to curriculum development that involves all stakeholders. When teachers design their own curriculum from the ground up, they are more likely to fully implement it.

Teacher collaboration to design the curriculum from the ground results in greater flexibility of teachers, increased student achievement, and more time spent teaching essential content and ideas. Grassroots curriculum development can also have a positive impact on the institution, including an increased sense of community, the development of a common philosophy, a greater emphasis on conceptual teaching, recognition of differences in teaching styles as a strength, increased team planning, and more meaningful professional development (Murata 2002).

When teachers continue to collaborate in teams about the application of the curriculum throughout the year, the implementation of the curriculum is more successful and student learning is enhanced. As a result of ongoing collaboration about the curriculum, teachers are able to learn from each other about what is working in their classrooms and are more likely to hold each other accountable for the curriculum.

Collaboration about curriculum and instruction has also been suggested to contribute to professional growth. It is unrealistic to assume that an individual teacher can meet the needs of thirty or more students without getting ideas from his or her colleagues on how to address the needs of the diverse learners. When teachers learn from their colleagues, studies suggest that their enthusiasm increases as they begin to feel more effective.

And, when teachers are involved in designing their own curriculum, they are more likely to take ownership of the teaching and learning of that curriculum as well; and their reflection and discussion about best practice improves. Teachers who were involved in grassroots curriculum development found that as they witnessed the dramatic outcomes in student achievement, they were motivated to invest more time and energy in their work. Teachers felt excited and invigorated by the creative process of designing and refining their curriculum (Murata 2002; Ozturk 2012).

They stated that, as a result, synergy and collaboration between both teachers and students increased, and students were influenced by the increased rapport between teachers (Murata 2002). Finally, although teachers feel more creative and autonomous when encouraged to take ownership of the curriculum, studies also indicate that teaching practices within schools become more aligned as well. With ownership comes buy-in, and when teachers have buy-in to the curriculum they are implementing they are more likely to hold each other accountable to deeply implementing the curriculum because they believe that it will have a positive impact on students.

Hattie's (2012) meta-meta analyses of education practices' effects on student outcome demonstrated that collaborative planning of curriculum and instruction among teachers has a higher likelihood of improving student achievement than most all other tasks in which teachers can partake. He asserts that this ownership and collaboration is essential to teachers developing a common understanding of the expectations for student learning and claims that teachers learn the craft by doing the work—not by hiring an outside expert to do it for them.

What is more, ongoing reflection and revision through teacher collaboration is more effective from a policy perspective than simply mandating curricula to teachers—even if that curriculum is of high quality. Curriculum creation and experimentation nurtures ownership and increases collaborative problem solving in institutions.

The process of collaboratively developing a curriculum from the ground up can also help to answer questions about the extent to which the standards are actually being taught in schools and can help all stakeholders in the institution become more clear on the goals for the learning. When teachers are mandated curricula in schools there is no guarantee that they will have an in-depth understanding of what students should know and be able to do.

However, when teachers are involved in the process of curriculum development, becoming familiar with the essential knowledge and skills that students must demonstrate is a prerequisite to their work. In this sense, the collaborative design of the curriculum becomes the glue that holds the teaching and learning in the institution together (Harden 2001).

Teacher ownership of the curriculum, however, is not the only essential component of a quality curriculum. Student ownership of the curriculum and the learning is also shown to increase achievement and motivation. When students feel autonomous and have choice in their learning, they are more likely to be motivated and engaged in the learning because they feel in control of their environment. Bishop and Plaum (2005) assert that students are curriculum theorists, whether or not we acknowledge it, and that it is important to draw them into the conversation about the purposes and practices of education as well.

A solid curriculum includes learning that is simultaneously relevant and rigorous. Students learn better when they can make connections and when they are challenged. The best curriculum is the one in which both students and teachers feel ownership because the resulting autonomy, creativity, and reflection are conducive to organic and ongoing learning. However, embracing grassroots curriculum design that fosters both relevance and rigor requires trust in educators as well as students.

While it is much easier for policymakers and educational leaders to simply purchase a curriculum and mandate fidelity in its implementation, this negates the expertise of educators, and, in turn, may make them feel as though they do not have great influence on the success of their students. Teachers may also feel less ownership of—and thus less buy-in to—what it is that students must know and be able to do, and they may not have an in-depth understanding of the knowledge and skills that students are expected to master.

However, when teachers are trusted with the process of curriculum design, they may become more invested in student learning as a result of their more in-depth understanding of the curriculum and increased commitment to continual reflection and revision throughout its implementation. This type of curriculum design demands time for ongoing dialogue among stakeholders in education about what skills provide students with the most leverage and what concepts and enduring understandings have the most potential to positively impact students and ultimately society.

If curriculum is so important for the success of students and the advancement of society, then it is crucial that educators and the public can articulate a common philosophy about what defines success and what our hopes are for our students and our society. Is economic superiority our aim? Is it personal fulfillment?

How can we begin to develop a relevant curriculum if we have not defined what is most relevant and important to us in the first place? Developing a curriculum that promotes the internal drive of our students is no easy task. However, we must trust in the abilities of our educators to do so, and we must provide them with the time and the resources to do it well.

IMPLICATIONS FOR INSTRUCTION

Knowing what to teach is only half of the battle in activating students' intrinsic drive. The second component of teaching and learning is the *how*—the actual instruction. The interplay between teacher and student and the dynamic of the classroom environment makes or breaks the learning of the curriculum. Instruction is ineffective without stimulating students' emotions. This is where the true challenge of teaching lies, and this is why some claim that teaching is more of an art than a science.

Once teachers have time, autonomy, and a strong sense of purpose, how do they go about doing the important work of optimizing students' intrinsic motivation and drive to learn? It might not even be possible if they are not masters of social and emotional intelligence to begin with or are not committed to developing in these areas. Thus, we need to reevaluate the criteria we use when hiring educators, and we need to rethink the professional development we provide teachers once they are hired.

A common sentiment among supervisors is that if they had to choose between substance (knowing your "stuff") and style (an ability to inspire and connect with others) they would choose substance. This seems backward. Substance is easier to learn than style. Technical skill is easier to acquire than social skill. Teachers are leaders of children. They must possess leadership qualities, and as we examined previously, the most influential leadership qualities are social and emotional skills.

Because teaching is a human and organic undertaking, once leaders are hired to teach our children, they must know themselves well. They must be aware of how their personalities and dispositions impact their students' engagement. A mandatory component of teachers' professional development should be self-assessment and reflection. Teachers' mind-sets, expectations, and beliefs have the largest impact on students' success. They are the hardest instructional components to impact from a coaching or supervisory standpoint.

Teachers should spend much of their time reflecting on how their core beliefs about students and about how their purpose in teaching translate into practice. And they should constantly be evaluating the costs and benefits of harboring such belief systems. Spiegel (2012) gives a concrete example of the cost of neglecting to examine our own belief systems and harboring low expectations for students.

Finding a Noble Purpose

In an experiment designed to examine the impact of teacher expectations on student achievement, teachers were told that some of their students had been given IQ tests that were designed to predict which students were on the verge of becoming very special—of achieving great things. The researchers chose students at random with varying levels of motivation and cognition and told teachers that these were the students who were about to go on to do great things.

Teachers began to treat these students differently. They begin to call on these students more, provide more wait time when they answered questions, gave them more feedback, and helped clarify their misunderstandings. And, to the researchers' astonishment, the fabricated prophecy was fulfilled: the students' IQs and achievement increased. Changing their expectations quite literally changed their students' abilities trajectory.

However, sometimes it is faster to change one's actions than to change one's core beliefs. Sometimes our core beliefs change when we see the positive results of our changed actions. For this reason, we need to provide teachers with the concrete skills and strategies to lead their students. And, the emphasis needs to be on *leading* their students, not simply managing them.

It is imperative that we change the narrative in schools from desiring effective "classroom management" to insisting on inspiring "classroom leadership." As adults, we expect to be led—to be inspired—not to be controlled or micromanaged. Yet, we often settle for less with our students. We accept that a quiet, orderly class is a good class regardless of whether the students are alive inside and passionate about their learning.

There is a great deal of research on effective leadership, and yet we do not often apply that wealth of knowledge to our classrooms. We continue to rely on extrinsic rewards and methods of control in order to get our students to behave and do their work rather than fostering the components in our teaching and in our classroom environment that fuel students' intrinsic drive.

Rewards have their place. They are not inherently evil. However, in the absence of true inspiration, the use of tangible rewards and consequences will only do so much to manage students. They will not awaken them to their passions and spark their deep-rooted motivation.

As mentioned previously, adults require more than carrot and stick measures to fuel our passion and motivation. We want to be autonomous in our workplace. We want to feel trusted and able to utilize our unique strengths and talents to get the job done. Students do too. As adults, we want to be sure that we are tasked with something that we actually possess the skills of and knowledge to complete and complete well. We want to know that we can become masters of our work. Students do too. Further, as adults we want our work to be meaningful so that it feels as though our efforts really contribute to this world and to others. Students do too.

The greatest way to activate adults' drive is by bringing meaning and emotion to the forefront of their work. The same is true for students. There are many ways we can foster meaning and purpose in our instruction. Our students who fall through the cracks do not do so because we have low standards, or because we have inferior resources and technology, or because we did not use the right curriculum.

Rather, our students fall through the cracks because we have not sustained their energy, excitement, and love for learning. "While we vigorously support high standards, rigorous curriculum, and emphasize critical thinking, problem solving, and intellectual scholarship for our students, we gain little if we have not stirred their hearts" (Maiers & Sandvold 2011, p. 1).

One study found that the most creative and passionate students in class were also the least favorite of most teachers. The students, however, who were rated as favorites of their teachers possessed traits such as conformity and unquestioning acceptance of authority. While ninety-five percent of teachers in the study said they value creativity, what they really valued in their classroom was compliance (Maiers & Sandvold 2011).

According to Maiers and Sandvold (2011), the best way to foster passion and motivation in the classroom is to commit to three simple ideals: show your passion as a teacher; know your students' passion, and bring their passion to the surface of the instruction and the learning; and understand and show how these passions can contribute to the various needs we have in the world.

A prerequisite to passion, however, is creating an ideal emotional atmosphere in classrooms and school buildings. Willis (2006) asserts, "We live in a stressful world in troubled times, and that is not supposed to be the way children grow up. School classrooms can be the safe haven where academic practices and classroom strategies can provide children with emotional comfort and pleasure as well as knowledge" (2006, p. 57).

Unfortunately, because standardized test results are linked to the financial stability of schools, the joy is stripped from many classrooms by third grade in an effort to achieve better student outcomes on those assessments. The problem is, however, that this thinking is misguided. When creativity is replaced with conformity and when joy is replaced with rote memorization, students' brains struggle to process the learning and store the learning in their long-term memories (Willis 2006).

On the other hand, the factors that have been shown to increase brain activity and information storage have more to do with students' comfort levels than time spent on concepts and skills. Factors such as self-confidence, trust, relationships with their teachers, and positive classroom and school environments are directly related to better understanding of the content, greater chance of retaining the learning, higher probability of making interdisciplinary connections, and the development of critical thinking skills (Willis 2006).

No objective neuroimaging or brain wave analysis data demonstrate any negative effects of joy and exuberance in classrooms, yet that has become the spoken or unspoken mandate. Now there is hard science that proves the negative brain impact of stress and anxiety and the beneficial changes in the brain that are seen when children are motivated by and personally connected to their lessons. . . . Even before the mandates catch up with the brain research, teachers are the frontline professionals who can use the techniques to keep this generation of students from failing into the abyss of joyless, factory-style education (Willis 2006, p. 59).

So, what does a classroom that activates students' internal drive look like? First and foremost, it is a low-stress environment. It has to be, given the levels of toxic stress with which many of our students enter school. Many schools across America are beginning to practice mindfulness and other strategies that promote students' social and emotional well-being in order to decrease their stress and provide them with the strategies and tools that will help them to thrive in life.

And surprisingly or not, schools that take the time to do this boast graduation rates that are fourteen percent higher than the national average, have students who enroll in college at a rate nine percent higher than the national average, and send students off to college who persist throughout their college careers at a rate of eighty-three percent (New Tech Network 2014).

Social and emotional learning cannot be separated from academic learning. One way to work on social development in schools is to develop the prefrontal cortex—the part of the brain that governs self-regulation. Some schools that are working with the most traumatized and disadvantaged students are implementing mindfulness programs in order to do so. Having students learn and practice centering techniques, such as focused breathing, can actually help students improve their focus and decision-making abilities.

One elementary school in Richmond, California, after just a few months of implementing a mindfulness program in their building, found that behavior problems diminished and academic achievement increased. And this is after having the students practice just a few minutes of mindfulness every week (Schwartz 2015).

This brings us back to the Marshmallow Experiment. Remember how Walter Mischel found that the more likely a child was to delay his gratification, the more likely he would be successful and happy later in life? Well, the good news is that self-control is like a muscle. The more we use it, the stronger it gets. If we want students to grow up to be successful, happy, productive citizens, we must exercise this muscle in schools. Practicing mindfulness is one way to do this.

Happiness experts outside of the field of education can offer more insight into how to foster children's well-being in schools. Achor (2011) suggests that the happiest people are those who practice gratitude, exercise, meditate, and engage in random acts of kindness. Is it possible to infuse these practices in our schools? Is it possible that doing so will not take away from the curriculum but allow students to better access it because their toxic stress will be addressed?

Biochemist turned Buddhist monk, Matthieu Ricard, says that it is possible to train our minds in habits of well-being—that it is possible to learn fulfillment (2004). He states that in the last twenty years or so we have learned that the brain is not fixed. The habits and abilities of our mind are pliable even in adulthood.

Just as an athlete or a musician becomes better the more she practices, the mind can slowly become better at developing the synapses that promote well-being the more we practice using positive emotional habits (Ricard 2004). What would happen if students spent time every day for the thirteen years of their kindergarten through twelfth grade experience practicing patience, delayed gratification, kindness, open-mindedness, and gratitude?

We do not have to look only to experts on well-being outside of education, though, to see how we might be able to implement these ideas in schools. School programs that aim to develop students' emotional well-being like PATHS (Promoting Alternative Thinking Strategies), FastTrack, and Ruler have shown promising results with students. Kenneth Dodge, a psychologist at Duke University, wanted to ascertain if programs such as these had lasting benefits with students. He wanted to see if teaching them social-emotional intelligence changed their life trajectory.

Thus, he conducted a study in which they screened five-year-olds in order to identify students who were most at risk for behavioral problems later in life. He had half of the students go through school as usual with access to the regular counseling and tutoring services they would normally have; the other half received social-emotional lessons from the PATHS program in addition to the normal school resources.

What he found was that by age twenty-five, students who received the social-emotional training had not only done better in school but they had fewer arrests and mental health and substance abuse issues later in life (Singh 2014). What's more, schools that focus on students' emotional well-being and provide students with strategies to improve their soft skills *in addition to* maintaining rigorous expectations for academic achievement have been shown to produce better test scores, stronger interpersonal and intrapersonal skills, greater opportunities to learn, and more equitable opportunities and outcomes (Garet et al. 2014).

So why don't most schools employ these programs or strategies if they are shown to be so beneficial to students and society *and* shown to increase test scores and prepare our students for the global economy? Mostly because they are expensive. Over a ten-year period, these programs can add up to $50,000 per student (Singh 2014). However, in the long run it will cost far less per child than juvenile detention centers, rehab programs, or incarceration. Wouldn't it be wiser to be proactive with our money in order to save tremendous amounts of money in the long run?

Even without funding, however, we can begin to make these changes. Jensen (2013) illustrates how. He states that there are five basic ways in which teachers can engage their students: by upgrading their attitudes; building relationships and respect with their students; getting buy-in from their students; embracing clarity in their instruction; and by showing their passion.

By embracing these five strategies, Jensen argues that teachers will find it much easier to implement various instructional strategies and curricula, and they will find that by using these strategies with whatever they implement, they will achieve their desired results because students' intrinsic drive will be stimulated. Jensen is a proponent of sweating the "small" stuff.

In order to carry out the noble mission of inspiring students and igniting their internal drive, everyone who serves in schools needs to sweat the small stuff. Because school culture and classroom culture are as important to student success as the instruction, and because it is our social and emotional skills that contribute to the greater school and classroom culture, we must be cognizant of every single interaction we have with others throughout every single day.

We need to focus on our own positivity as teachers if students' positivity is critical to their success. We need to cultivate personal relationships with our students and our staff. We need to engage in professional development around our social and emotional skills as all the nuances in our body language and our behavior in the classroom and in the school add up to create a big impact on students' and staff's motivation and positivity.

Finally, we have focused so much on rigor in public education that we have forgotten the importance of joy. Rigor and joy are not mutually exclusive. They are interdependent. It is time to infuse our classrooms and our curriculum with joy. It is time to bring the fun back into the learning. If we are looking to our students to become future innovators of the world, surely we must show them how much fun innovation can be. Our teachers should be smiling. Our students should be smiling. They should be smiling because if we don't leverage their happiness and hope now, we won't have much chance for improving our future.

Do not mistake, however, prioritizing students' social and emotional well-being in schools with keeping students comfortable or making their learning and their life easy. American author, Neale Donald Walsch (2010), once said that "life begins at the end of your comfort zone." No truer words have been spoken. Focusing on students' well-being and intrinsic drive are not excuses for making the learning less challenging or for expecting less of them in general.

In fact, challenge is an essential factor in motivation to learn. We need to push our students outside their comfort zones while simultaneously feeding their spirits. Every good parent knows that keeping his or her child happy at all costs will not a happy grown-up make. Rather, a child who never experiences struggle or pain likely grows up to take much for granted and act entitled. On the contrary, a child who is expected to behave well, is held accountable for her actions, and is frequently pushed to the limits of her comfort zone will gain confidence, learn responsibility and self-discipline, and ultimately grow up to be happier.

Good parents also know that they must balance that pressure with support. They must use positive reinforcement more than redirection or negative reinforcement. They must model positive behavior, positive interaction with others, and foster a growth mind-set. The truth is that many of our students' parents lack the skill sets necessary to ensure that their children come to school prepared to learn.

Many of our students come into our schools with toxic stress and severely underdeveloped soft skills. We cannot simply push them out of their comfort zones when they walk through our doors and apply more pressure in their lives without concurrently working to reduce their stress and improve their social and emotional skills. School may be the only place where many of our students experience positive relationships; and we cannot underestimate the power of that human connection.

However, it is not enough to simply know our mission and how to carry it out if we do not have the tools, resources, and ability to actually see it to fruition. In addition to paying teachers what they are worth, we need to set the stage for an optimal work environment. One of the biggest complaints that teachers have regarding their inability to achieve success with their students is lack of time.

Imagine you are told that tomorrow you will be presenting at a conference for six hours in a room full of people who have varying levels of understanding about the topic you are presenting and varying levels of interest in it. However, you are expected to engage all conference participants for the entire six hours. Your evaluation and your pay will be determined on their level of engagement. Now imagine that I told you that you had only a half hour to plan that conference.

This is the pressure many of our teachers feel every day. Only they aren't simply given a half an hour to prepare for one days' worth of learning. They are tasked with this insurmountable chore every day of the school year. Some teachers are even told to do this without any resources whatsoever. Would you be able to plan six hours of meaningful and inspiring learning in a half hour's time and be able to develop the curriculum for those six hours yourself? Additionally, would you be able to provide meaningful and timely feedback to your students?

What we are essentially saying to educators is, "Please fix society. And, by the way . . . wing it." It is ridiculous. We would demand more as adult learners, and we should demand more for our children. Teaching is incredibly complex and difficult. Why do we assume that we can realize our purpose in education without the proper time and tools to do so?

Finally, we must reward teachers' efforts and innovation, not just their results. Much research illustrates the importance of praising effort over achievement. When we praise the efforts of others, their achievement actually increases because they are more likely to adopt a growth mind-set and believe that their hard work will pay off. However, when we praise someone's achievement, she often attributes her success to inherent intelligence or skill and not work ethic or creativity and is more inclined to take fewer risks in her efforts to achieve, resulting in lower achievement in the future.

What's more, because teaching is complex, it's likely that many teachers are not sure what factors contributed to their success or failure in the first place, so simply rewarding or punishing them based on their achievements does not accomplish much, as they do not know how to replicate their success or avoid future failure. However, if we praise teachers' efforts and innovations in their classroom, they understand what to continue to do more of, and that leads to increased success in the future.

According to Chenoweth (2015), a synthesis of the factors that produce unprecedented student achievement in schools revealed the following characteristics: an unwavering focus on what students need to learn most; teachers' collaboration around unit, lesson, and assessment design; the use of formative assessment to drive instruction; and finally, *a culture of trust between students, teachers, administrators, and parents.* We cannot overlook this last factor simply because it is less tangible than the others.

IMPLICATIONS FOR SOCIETY

According to the Child Development Institute (n.d.), if students' social and emotional needs at any stage in their development go unmet, they cannot enter the next stage of development with the abilities to navigate the new social/emotional territory. For example, an infant's primary social and emotional needs are to be handled, nurtured, and loved.

When these needs are met, children develop trust and security, and the foundation of their hope and well-being is set. They are then prepared to move onto the next stage of their development where they negotiate their independence and fulfill their toddler desire of autonomy. If, however, these needs to be loved and nurtured go unmet, the infant becomes insecure and struggles to develop relationships and trust others. Without this self-assurance and feeling of connection to others, the child is not prepared to navigate the next stage of development—exerting his independence—because he is still focused on meeting his basic needs of love and connection.

There are many of these social/emotional stages that children navigate through life. Throughout the course of childhood, children must learn how to trust and connect to others; they must exert their independence and become confident in their ability to have some control over their environments; they must broaden their skills through play; they must learn self-discipline and how to relate to peers; and eventually they must experiment with their identity in order to develop a positive sense of self.

If their needs go unmet in any of these stages, or if these stages are rife with toxic stress rather than support and encouragement, the child's entire development is halted. He becomes stuck in that stage of social/emotional development and stuck socially and emotionally. The implications of this are monumental. Consider that many children—especially our children from poverty—enter school with toxic stress, riddled with insecurity and distrust because their initial need of being nurtured was not met.

Thus, many of our students are stuck in this stage of negotiating how to acquire attention—how to connect with others. Although we as educators and society expect them to have moved through this first stage and the handful of developmental stages after, they are nowhere near the self-discipline stage we expect them to be in. They are all but screaming to be loved when they walk through the doors of our schools.

Yet, the symptoms of their poor development are explosive behavior, disrespect, defiance, and lack of focus on academics. Because we have not made their well-being a priority and because we do not have the tools to address it even if we did, we tell them to sit down, get quiet, and get ready for learning.

Since the dawn of public education in America, citizens have held onto the idea of the common school—a system of public education that is truly equitable for all children and acts as a social equalizer for society. Over the course of U.S. history we have tried to promote equity in education by addressing disparities in opportunity based on race, gender, ability, and income.

We have addressed these disparities by attempting to ensure that the learning is equally accessible to all students regardless of their culture, ethnicity, language, geography, and socioeconomic status. While we have made significant progress in these areas in schools and in society, we are nowhere close to realizing our vision of the common school.

Maybe this is because we are focusing on the wrong thing. Maybe we have held the wrong purpose for education all along. Maybe the achievement gap in schools is more reflective of a gap in inspiration than a gap in academics. Maybe the way to address equity in education is to address children's well-being—to counteract their toxic stress—and to give them hope.

We must address their human needs in order for us to address their academic needs. In doing so, we can activate their internal drive. The sweet spot of learning seems to be at the intersection of academics, soft skills, and internal drive (see illustration on page 125). If we spend our time in public education in this sweet spot, students will leave school "college and career ready." More importantly, they will leave school empowered by the deep belief that they matter in this world.

What would happen to our dropout rate if we had students who cared and who were inspired? Students who drop out do so because they are hopeless. So, let's give them hope, not merely math and reading skills. What would happen to our workforce if students left their K–12 experience in schools empowered and hopeful? Would employers have the same concerns about employees' work ethic, or would those current shortcomings and soft skills already have been addressed in the school system?

What would happen to our society if we tackled poverty not only by attempting to address the income gap but also by attempting to address the inspiration gap as well? What would happen to society if we focused as much on meeting students' basic human needs as we do on competing in the global economy? Do we need to debate the true purpose of education, or is it true that regardless of our desires for public education the activation of students' internal drive will ultimately lead to the realization of all our aims? As argued by Robinson,

> You take an area, a school, a district, you change the conditions, give people a different sense of possibility, a different set of expectations, a broader range of opportunities, you cherish and value the relationships between teachers and learners, you offer people the discretion to be creative and to innovate in what they do, and schools that were once bereft spring to life. . . . The real role of leadership is climate control, creating a climate of possibility. And if you do that, people will rise to it and achieve things that you completely did not anticipate and couldn't have expected (2013, 16:34).

Chapter 6

Conclusion

The principal smiled at me from across the table. "You wanted to meet with me about David?" he asked.

"Yes," I replied. "I'm concerned about the results of his motivation assessment combined with his lack of growth in reading. I wanted to update you on a brainstorming session I had with his parents last week."

I had had my eye on David for the last few months. Something wasn't quite right. Not only had his growth in reading plateaued, but it seemed this plateau was a symptom of an even larger problem: David didn't seem to be enjoying school. It wasn't just a hunch, though. The results of our monthly intrinsic drive assessments indicated that David was struggling in the areas of significance and contribution.

According to the student survey, David wasn't feeling as though he had anything of value to offer his class and his school. He didn't feel like his school or classroom was enhanced by his efforts or even his attendance, so motivation slowly gave way to apathy, and he had spent much of his time lately just getting through each day. This was a red flag that wasn't to be taken lightly.

The good news was that David's soft skills were intact. He worked well with his peers, was able to stay organized in class, and even embraced a growth mind-set: He understood that it was his effort—not his intelligence—that ultimately led to success. The root of the problem, according to the data, was that he simply wasn't inspired to put much effort forth lately. I had been working hard at making my reading lessons engaging to the class and, at least during the lessons themselves, David was fairly engaged.

It wasn't that David didn't have the strategies to become a better reader. It was more that he spent his independent reading time staring out the window or slumped over on his desk. If we could engage him in independent reading then he would naturally move forward in reading levels due to the daily practice. Fortunately, his family and I had come up with a plan that we thought might address the origin of his disengagement.

David did, in fact, have a lot to offer others in terms of contribution. Where David truly shined was in his interactions with younger kids. He was frequently seen helping the younger children at recess when they were hurt or upset. He also had a kindergarten sister who attended our school whom he adored, and he took his role as big brother very seriously.

David mattered. And it wasn't just his achievement as a reader that made him matter. His kindness toward others was an asset to our school culture, and his service as a role model and mentor to younger students was invaluable. We knew it, but apparently David did not. Thus, his family and I came up with a plan to help him realize that he mattered and had something to offer since these were areas of need that were currently not being met.

We decided to ask David if he would read to a second-grade girl who could use some support in reading as well as a strong role model and friend. Each day while the rest of the class was reading independently in their choice reading books, David would take his book box to her second-grade class and read to her. Hopefully, this responsibility would help David to feel not only that he mattered and had something to offer, but it would also inspire him to invest in his own reading development as he would have an authentic and relevant reason to improve.

I explained our plan to the principal as he nodded and asked a few questions. "I'm glad we are catching this now," he responded when I was finished articulating the specifics of the proposal.

> This is a critical time in David's life and his schooling. His future success depends on his feelings about school and his feelings about himself. Your class will be taking the end-of-year standardized assessment in a few weeks.
>
> Let's hope that David's score reflects his ability and level of motivation at that time so that we can continue to get him the help he needs and advocate for him. If he has improved and found confidence as a reader, a good score on the test will surely serve as validation for us that he is growing as a learner. If his scores come back as worrisome, we will be able to use that data as a reason to continue this conversation with his parents and the intervention team about how we can better meet his needs.

I thanked my boss for his interest in David and his laser-like focus on improving our students' intrinsic drive to learn. I left the meeting feeling hopeful that David would get back on track as a reader and would begin to engage in school again because he would know that the unique talents he brings to the table are important in this world. It wasn't just David, though, who would feel like he mattered as a result of fostering this noble purpose for education. I, too, felt like my contributions mattered. While teaching was certainly no easy task, it was worth it. I woke up every morning inspired by a mission that I knew was essential to the betterment of these kids and their future.

I left our meeting and walked down the halls lined with student drawings and paintings. I peeked in rooms full of joy where students were hovering with pride over their work. I knew the rigor and relevance these teachers were fostering in their rooms because I had worked with them to design the curriculum. It was truly exciting stuff.

In the drama wing, I spotted students filming the storyline of a math word problem they were attempting to understand. Understanding the problems was half of the battle but when students had the ability to act them out, the math came to life. In the art room students were painting a metaphor that served to represent their favorite character from a novel they just finished. Their metaphors not only required critical thinking skills to develop but their paintings required learning many engaging art techniques as well.

In the engineering wing, students were using real world math to work on a design for the cafeteria that would make getting food at lunch more efficient within the financial constraints of the project and physical constraints of the space. This project was certainly relevant to students as it was an issue they dealt with every day. And in the community service wing, students were writing persuasive essays to the local community center convincing it to remain open on Saturdays. After doing research, they were able to cite many valid reasons why opening the community center on Saturdays would benefit the children and families in the town.

These students truly felt like they were making a difference in their community, and they definitely were learning research and communication skills that would benefit them later in life. Since we are working on the supreme standard of "expressing our feelings respectfully" in class, we had been sending homework home in that area. In addition to their daily reading and math, students were to practice taking deep breaths when they felt frustrated and then, when calm enough, they were to use "I statements," such as "I feel frustrated when you tell me 'no' all the time before even considering what I'm asking."

Because we often align our supreme standards that we are working on in class with our focus for our PTA meetings, we truly are working hard to become a village for these children, and our parents really appreciate it. I had already received a handful of emails from families who found that by focusing on respectfully expressing their feelings, their interactions have become more positive, and everyone in the family seems calmer and less stressed.

I smiled acknowledging a thought that often crept into my mind as I meandered through these halls: *I get PAID to do this?* I couldn't imagine more fulfilling work. Just yesterday at a PTA meeting I had the opportunity to work with families to explore more research and strategies that could be used to improve their interactions with their children and bring some peace back into their homes.

The free childcare and dinner that was offered at the biweekly meetings certainly helped bring in families. Families also flocked to take advantage of the many resources we provided. We always had stations where local medical care providers, nutritionists, and social workers were available for families to network with and gather resources.

Often times we had community members who took part in our discussions and focus groups during our meetings.

Law enforcement officers could frequently be seen working side by side with families to determine proactive ways to help their children make positive decisions. This collaboration had made a huge impact in our community. Everyone knew the children and their families. There was a sense of purpose and togetherness that infused every interaction in our "hub."

This sense of togetherness is what had overwhelmed me and brought me to tears a few months back at one of our meetings. We had spent many previous meetings discussing the impact and importance of focusing on at least three positives to every negative when interacting with children, and this week's meeting was a share-out on how it had been working for families.

A parent of two of our most struggling students had been quiet during the share-out session. I had sensed that she was still struggling to find her voice and her confidence in the school community. Schools didn't operate like this when she grew up, and she still had negative feelings about schools that we were working hard to change. When the meeting finished, however, I saw one of our local police officers approach her and ask about her son who has struggled quite a bit in the past with making positive choices. His motivation assessments had indicated for years he struggled in the area of significance, and despite all of our efforts in school he still struggled to feel fulfilled in this area.

The mother of this child looked as if she was about to cry. "You cannot believe what a difference I see in my son. He seems lighter . . . less defensive and less likely to act out at home. Do you think it could really be the effort I have put into using more positive comments with him over the past few months?"

"It certainly couldn't have hurt," the officer responded. "He's a great kid deep down. We are going to get there with him. You'll see. With so many people invested in his well-being, he's going to realize eventually that we all care very much. He has it in him to become great. He really does." At that point the mother collapsed into the officer's arms and started sobbing. "Thank you," she muttered. "Thank you."

Witnessing this moment profoundly changed me as an educator. It can sometimes feel overwhelming shouldering the responsibility of growing human beings. But, I realized I wasn't in it alone. The entire community had come together under a purpose that moved us to do and be our best for these children, and it was making a difference. It really was. After all, it was truly what was best for kids.

Appendix

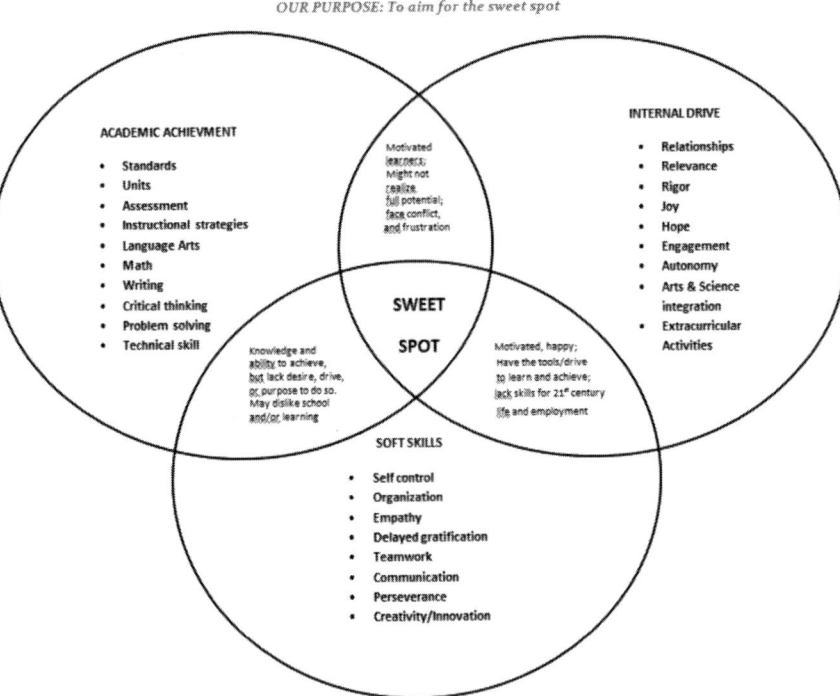

Bibliography

Achor, Shawn. "The Happy Secret to Better Work." *TED Talks* (2011).

Ackerman, David B. "Taproots for a New Century: Tapping the Best of Traditional and Progressive Education." *Phi Delta Kappan* 84, no. 5 (2003): 344–349. doi: 10.1177/003172170308400505.

Adkins, Amy. "U.S. Employee Engagement Reaches Three-Year High." U.S. Employee Engagement Reaches Three-Year High. Accessed May 17, 2015. http://www.gallup.com/poll/181895/employee-engagement-reaches-three-year-high.aspx?utm_source=alert&utm_medium=email&utm_content=heading&utm_campaign=syndication.

Amat, Jose A., Ravi Bansal, Ronald Whiteman, Rita Haggerty, Jason Royal, and Bradley S. Peterson. "Correlates of Intellectual Ability with Morphology of the Hippocampus and Amygdala in Healthy Adults." *Brain and Cognition* 66, no. 2 (2008): 105–14. doi: 10.1016/j.bandc.2007.05.009.

Anderson, Richard C., Kim Nguyen-Jahiel, Brian Mcnurlen, Anthi Archodidou, So-Young Kim, Alina Reznitskaya, Maria Tillmanns, and Laurie Gilbert. "The Snowball Phenomenon: Spread of Ways of Talking and Ways of Thinking Across Groups of Children." *Cognition and Instruction* 19, no. 1 (2001): 1–46. doi: 10.1207/s1532690xci1901_1.

Anderson, Kim, Tiffany Harrison, and Karla Lewis. "Plans to Adopt and Implement Common Core State Standards in the Southeast Region States. Issues & Answers. REL 2012-No. 136." *Regional Educational Laboratory Southeast* (2012).

Ariely, Dan, Emir Kamenica, and Dražen Prelec. "Man's Search for Meaning: The Case of Legos." *Journal of Economic Behavior & Organization* 67, no. 3 (2008): 671–677.

Ariely, Dan. "What Makes Us Feel Good about Our Work?" *TED Talks* (2010).

Beane, James A. "Common Core of a Different Sort: Putting Democracy at the Center of the Curriculum." *Middle School Journal (J3)* 44, no. 3 (2013): 6–14.

Benade, Leon. "A Critical Review of Curriculum Mapping: Implications for the Development of an Ethical Teacher Professionally." *New Zealand Journal of Teachers' Work* 5, no. 2 (2008): 93–104.

Biesta, Gert. "Good Education in an Age of Measurement: On the Need to Reconnect with the Question of Purpose in Education." *Educational Assessment, Evaluation and Accountability* 21, no. 1 (2008): 33–46. doi: 10.1007/s11092-008-9064-9.

Bill & Melinda Gates Foundation. "Asking Students About Teaching." *Met Project* (2013). http://www.metproject.org/dowloads/Asking_Students_Summary_Doc.pdf.

Bishaw, Alemayehu, and Trudi J. Renwick. "Poverty: 2007 and 2008 American Community Surveys." *American Community Survey Report ACSBR/08-1. Washington, DC: US Census Bureau* (2011).

Bishop, Penny A., and Susanna W. Pflaum. "Student Perceptions of Action, Relevance, and Pace." *Middle School Journal (J1)* 36, no. 4 (2005): 4–12.

Blackwell, Lisa S., Kali H. Trzesniewski, and Carol Sorich Dweck. "Implicit Theories of Intelligence Predict Achievement Across an Adolescent Transition: A Longitudinal Study and an Intervention." *Child Development* 78, no. 1 (2007): 246–63. doi: 10.1111/j.1467-8624.2007.00995.x.

Boerema, Albert J. "Does Mission Matter? An Analysis of Private School Achievement Differences." *Journal of School Choice* 3, no. 2 (2009): 112–37. doi: 10.1080/15582150902996708.

Boutin, James. "An Urban Teacher's Education: Wait! I'm a Radical Educator?" Accessed May 17, 2015. http://www.anurbanteacherseducation.com/2014/12/wait-im-radical-educator.html.

Bracey, Gerald W. "Poverty's Infernal Mechanism." *Principal Leadership* 6, no. 6 (2006): 60.

Bradley, Robert H., and Robert F. Corwyn. "Socioeconomic Status and Child Development." *Annual Review of Psychology* 53, no. 1 (2002): 371–99. doi: 10.1146/annurev.psych.53.100901.135233.

Brinegar, Kathleen, and Penny A. Bishop. "Student Learning and Engagement in the Context of Curriculum Integration." *Middle Grades Research Journal* 6, no. 4 (2011): 207–222.

Buckingham, Marcus, and Ashley Goodall. "Reinventing Performance Management." *Harvard Business Review*, April (2015).

Carmichael, Sheila Byrd, Gabrielle Martino, Kathleen Porter-Magee, and W. Stephen Wilson. "The State of State Standards–and the Common Core–in 2010." *Thomas B. Fordham Institute* (2010).

Carnevale, Anthony P., Jeff Strohl, and Nicole Smith. "Help Wanted: Postsecondary Education and Training Required." *New Directions for Community Colleges* 2009, no. 146 (2009): 21–31. doi: 10.1002/cc.363.

Carpenter, Dick M. "Gubernatorial Rhetoric and the Purpose of Education in the United States." *International Journal of Education Policy and Leadership* 6, no. 6 (2011).

Carr-Chellman, Ali. "Gaming to Re-engage Boys in Learning." *TED Talks* (2010).

Chenoweth, Karin. "Improving Schools: What Works?: How Do We Get from Here to There?" *Educational Leadership* 72, no. 5 (February 2015). Accessed April 10, 2015. http://www.ascd.org/publications/educational-leadership/feb15/vol72/num05/Five-Myths-About-School-Improvement.aspx.

Child Development Institute. "Know What to Expect! The 8 Stages of Social Development in Children." Accessed May 17, 2015. http://childdevelopmentinfo.com/child-development/erickson/.

Childre, Amy, Jennifer R. Sands, and Saundra Tanner Pope. "Backward Design." *Teaching Exceptional Children* 41, no. 5 (2009): 6–14.

Choppin, Jeffrey. "Learned Adaptations: Teachers' Understanding and Use of Curriculum Resources." *Journal of Mathematics Teacher Education* 14, no. 5 (2011): 331–53. doi: 10.1007/s10857-011-9170-3.

Choppin, Jeffrey Martin. "Curriculum-Context Knowledge: Teacher Learning from Successive Enactments of a Standards-Based Mathematics Curriculum." *Curriculum Inquiry* 39, no. 2 (2009): 287–320. doi: 10.1111/j.1467-873x.2009.00444.x.

Clark, Ann-Marie, Richard C. Anderson, Li-jen Kuo, Il-Hee Kim, Anthi Archodidou, and Kim Nguyen-Jahiel. "Collaborative Reasoning: Expanding Ways for Children to Talk and Think in School." *Educational Psychology Review* 15, no. 2 (2003): 181–198.

Cohen, Jeff. "Two Years Later, Still Learning from Sandy Hook." *NPR*. Accessed May 17, 2015. http://www.npr.org/2014/12/14/370378176/two-years-later-still-learning-from-sandy-hook. National Governors Association. "Common Core State Standards" (2010).

Common Core State Standards Initiative. "Development Process." *Development Process*. Accessed May 23, 2015. http://www.corestandards.org/about-the-standards/development-process/.

Conley, David. "Building on the Common Core." *Educational Leadership* 68, no. 6 (2011). http://ascd.org.

Counts, George S. "Excerpts from Dare the School Build a New Social Order? (1932)*." *Schools: Studies in Education* 10, no. 2 (2013): 281–88. doi: 10.1086/673335.

Csikszentmihalyi, Mihaly. *Flow: The Psychology of Optimal Experience*. New York: Harper & Row, 1990.

De Cos Patricia. *California's Public Schools: What Experts Say about Their Mission and Functions*. Sacramento, CA: California State Library, California Research Bureau, 2001.

Dean, Ceri B., Elizabeth Ross Hubbell, Howard Pitler, BJ Stone, and Robert J. Marzano. *Classroom Instruction That Works: Research-based Strategies for Increasing Student Achievement*. Alexandria, VA: ASCD, 2012.

DeNisco, Alison. "Ed Group Wants to Halt High-stakes Testing for Evaluations." *District Administration Magazine*. Accessed May 17, 2015. http://www.districtadministration.com/article/ed-group-wants-halt-high-stakes-testing-evaluations.

Deresiewicz, William. *Excellent Sheep: The Miseducation of the American Elite and the Way to a Meaningful Life*. Simon & Schuster, 2014.

Diener, Ed, Weiting Ng, James Harter, and Raksha Arora. "Wealth and Happiness across the World: Material Prosperity Predicts Life Evaluation, Whereas Psychosocial Prosperity Predicts Positive Feeling." *Journal of Personality and Social Psychology* 99, no. 1 (2010): 52–61. doi: 10.1037/a0018066.

Dobyns, Lydia. "Soft Skills Are 'Hard as a Rock'" *The Huffington Post*. Accessed May 17, 2015. http://www.huffingtonpost.com/lydia-dobyns/soft-skills-are-hard-as-a_b_3541023.html.

Doig, Brian, and Susie Groves. "Japanese Lesson Study: Teacher Professional Development through Communities of Inquiry." *Mathematics Teacher Education and Development* 13, no. 1 (2011): 77–93.

Duckworth, Angela. "The Key to Success? Grit." Angela Lee Duckworth. *TED Talks* (2013).

Dweck, Carol. *Mindset: The New Psychology of Success*. New York: Random House, 2006.
Einhorn, Erin. "Rich School, Poor School." *NPR*. Accessed May 17, 2015. http://www.npr.org/blogs/ed/2015/02/09/382122276/rich-school-poor-school.
Ellsworth, James B., Philip R. Harris, and Stephanie L. Moore. "The Purpose Project: Of School Reform, Covey, and Sun Tzu: The Conversation Begins." *TechTrends* 55, no. 5 (2011): 20–23. doi: 10.1007/s11528-011-0523-7.
Emery, Robert E., and Lisa Laumann-Billings. "An Overview of the Nature, Causes, and Consequences of Abusive Family Relationships: Toward Differentiating Maltreatment and Violence." *American Psychologist* 53, no. 2 (1998): 121–135. doi: 10.1037//0003-066x.53.2.121.
Ferrero, David. "Having It All." *Educational Leadership* 63, no. 8 (2006).
Fischer, Claude, and Michael Schudson. "The Good Citizen: A History of American Civic Life." *Contemporary Sociology* 29, no. 5 (2000): 741. doi: 10.2307/2655260.
Flannery, Mary Ellen. "The School to Prison Pipeline: Time to Shut It Down." *NEA Today* 33, no. 4 (2015): 42–45. Accessed April 2, 2015. http://neatoday.org.
Gallup. "Gallup Student Poll 2014 U.S. Overall Report." Gallup Student Poll 2014 U.S. Overall Report. Accessed May 17, 2015. http://www.gallup.com/services/180029/gallup-student-poll-2014-overall-report.aspx.
Gardner, Howard. "Beyond Wit & Grit: Howard Gardner's '8 for 8'" *YouTube*. Accessed May 17, 2015. http://www.youtube.com/watch?v=vnqWZdcC8AE.
Garet, Michael, Jordan Rickles, Michael Segeritz, James Taylor, and Kristina Zeiser. "Evidence of Deeper Learning Outcomes." September 2014. Accessed April 2015. www.air.org/sites/default/files/dowloads/reports/Report_3_Evidence_of_Deeper_Learning_Outcomes.pdf.
Garland, Sarah. "The Man behind Common Core Math." *NPR*. Accessed May 17, 2015. http://www.npr.org/blogs/ed/2014/12/29/371918272/the-man-behind-common-core-math.
Garmston, Robert J., and Arthur L. Costa. "Cognitive Coaching SM: A Foundation for Renaissance Schools" (2002).
Gates, Bill. "Mosquitos, Malaria and Education." *TED Talks* (2009).
Geller, Scott. "Watch the Psychology of Self-Motivation." *TED Talks* (2015).
Gershoff, Elizabeth Thompson. "Corporal Punishment by Parents and Associated Child Behaviors and Experiences: A Meta-analytic and Theoretical Review." *Psychological Bulletin* 128, no. 4 (2002): 539–579. doi: 10.1037/0033-2909.128.4.539.
Goleman, Daniel. "Daniel Goleman Explains Emotional Intelligence." *YouTube*. Accessed May 17, 2015. http://www.youtube.com/watch?v=ZsdqBC1tHTA.
Goleman, Daniel, and Richard Boyatzis. "Social Intelligence and the Biology of Leadership." *Harvard Business Review* 86, no. 9 (2008): 74–81.
Goodson, Ivor. "All the Lonely People: The Struggle for Private Meaning and Public Purpose in Education." *Critical Studies in Education* 48, no. 1 (2007): 131–148. doi: 10.1080/17508480601120954.
Graff, Nelson. "An Effective and Agonizing Way to Learn": Backwards Design and New Teachers' Preparation for Planning Curriculum." *Teacher Education Quarterly* (2011): 151–168.

Halstead, Jeff. *Navigating the New Pedagogy: Six Principles that Transform Teaching*. R&L Education, 2011.

Hanson, Jamie L., Amitabh Chandra, Barbara L. Wolfe, and Seth D. Pollak. "Association between Income and the Hippocampus." *PLoS ONE* 6, no. 5 (2011). doi: 10.1371/journal.pone.0018712.

Harden, R. M. "AMEE Guide No. 21: Curriculum Mapping: A Tool for Transparent and Authentic Teaching and Learning." *Med Teach Medical Teacher* 23, no. 2 (2001): 123–137. doi: 10.1080/01421590120036547.

Hari, Johann. "The Likely Cause of Addiction Has Been Discovered, and It Is Not What You Think." *The Huffington Post*. Accessed May 17, 2015. http://www.huffingtonpost.com/johann-hari/the-real-cause-of-addicti_b_6506936.html.

Hart, Betty, and Todd R. Risley. *Meaningful Differences in the Everyday Experience of Young American Children*. Baltimore, MD: Paul H. Brookes Publishing, 1995.

Hattie, John. *Visible Learning: A Synthesis of Over 800 Meta-analyses Relating to Achievement*. New York: Routledge, 2013.

Henry, Paul C. "Life Stresses, Explanatory Style, Hopelessness, and Occupational Class." *International Journal of Stress Management* 12, no. 3 (2005): 241–256. doi: 10.1037/1072-5245.12.3.241.

Hoggart, Keith. "Developing a Growth Mindset in Teachers and Staff." *Edutopia*. Accessed May 17, 2015. http://www.edutopia.org/discussion/developing-growth-mindset-teachers-and-staff.

Hough, Lory. "What's Worth Learning in School?" *Harvard Graduate School of Education*. Accessed May 17, 2015. http://www.gse.harvard.edu/news/ed/15/01/whats-worth-learning-school.

Houghton Mifflin Harcourt. "Assessment 101: PARCC & SBAC." Accessed April 2015. http://www.hmhco.com/educators/education-topics/by-topic/common-core/assessment-101-PARCC-and-SBAC.

Jensen, Eric. *Engaging Students with Poverty in Mind: Practical Strategies for Raising Achievement*. ASCD, 2013.

Kalb, Loretta. "Mindfulness Practices Buoy Students in Sacramento's Einstein Middle School." *Sacbee*. Accessed May 17, 2015. http://www.sacbee.com/news/local/education/article9531740.html.

Kamenetz, Anya. "A New Study Reveals Much about How Parents Really Choose Schools." *NPR*. Accessed May 17, 2015. http://www.npr.org/blogs/ed/2015/01/15/376966406/a-new-study-reveals-much-about-how-parents-really-choose-schools.

Kamenetz, Anya. "What Schools Could Use Instead of Standardized Tests." *NPR*. Accessed May 17, 2015. http://www.npr.org/blogs/ed/2015/01/06/371659141/what-schools-could-use-instead-of-standardized-tests.

Keeny, Michael. "School Leadership 2.0." Virginia Teacher of the Year Tells Why He Resigned. Accessed May 17, 2015. http://www.schoolleadership20.com/m/blogpost?id=1990010%3ABlogPost%3A205389.

Kinniburgh, Leah H., and Kelly Byrd. "Ten Black Dots and September 11: Integrating Social Studies and Mathematics through Children's Literature." *The Social Studies* 99, no. 1 (2008): 33–36. doi: 10.3200/tsss.99.1.33–36.

Konnikova, Maria. "Walter Mischel, the Marshallow Test, and Self-Control-The New Yorker." *The New Yorker*. October 09, 2014. Accessed May 17, 2015. http://www.newyorker.com/science/maria-konnikova/struggles-psychologist-studying-self-control.
Konnikova, Maria. "How Children Learn to Read-The New Yorker." *The New Yorker*. February 11, 2015. Accessed May 17, 2015. http://www.newyorker.com/science/maria-konnikova/how-children-learn-read.
Kuhn, Deanna. "Thinking as Argument." *Critical Readings on Piaget*, 1996, 120–46. doi: 10.4324/9780203435854_chapter_7.
Lam, Dianne, Pon Radhakrishnan, and Ulrich Shimmack. "Repeatedly Answering Questions That Elicit Inquiry-Based Thinking Improves Writing." *Journal of Instructional Psychology* 38, no. 4 (2011): 247–252.
Lam, Tak Shing. "Deliberation and School Based Curriculum Development—A Hong Kong Case Study." *New Horizons in Education* 59, no. 2 (2011): 69–82.
Lamie, Judith M. "Presenting a Model of Change." *Lang Teach Res Language Teaching Research* 8, no. 2 (2004): 115–142. doi: 10.1191/1362168804lr137oa.
Law, Edmond H. F., Sally W. Y. Wan, Maurice Galton, and John C. K. Lee. "Managing School-based Curriculum Innovations: A Hong Kong Case Study." *The Curriculum Journal* 21, no. 3 (2010): 313–32. doi: 10.1080/09585176.2010.504577.
Lee, James O. "Reach Teachers Now to Ensure Common Core Success." *Phi Delta Kappan* 92, no. 6 (2011): 42–44. doi: 10.1177/003172171109200609.
Leipzig, Adam. "Watch How to Know Your Life Purpose in 5 Minutes." *TED Talks* (2014).
Lesley, Mellinee. "Exploring the Links between Critical Literacy and Developmental Reading." *Journal of Adolescent & Adult Literacy* 45, no. 3 (2001): 180–189.
Lichter, Daniel T. "Poverty and Inequality among Children." *Annual Review of Sociology* 23, no. 1 (1997): 121–45. doi: 10.1146/annurev.soc.23.1.121.
MacDonald, Fiona. "No More Physics and Maths, Finland to Stop Teaching Individual Subjects." *ScienceAlert*. Accessed May 17, 2015. http://www.sciencealert.com/no-more-physics-and-maths-finland-to-stop-teaching-individual-subjects.
Macmath, Sheryl, Jillian Roberts, John Wallace, and Xiaohong Chi. "Curriculum Integration and At-risk Students: A Canadian Case Study Examining Student Learning and Motivation." *British Journal of Special Education* 37, no. 2 (2010): 87–94. doi: 10.1111/j.1467-8578.2009.00454.x.
Maiers, Angela, and Amy Sandvold. *The Passion-driven Classroom: A Framework for Teaching & Learning*. Larchmont, NY: Eye on Education, 2010.
Malatesta, Carol Z., Carol E. Izard, Clayton Culver, and Mark Nicolich. "Emotion Communication Skills in Young, Middle-aged, and Older Women." *Psychology and Aging* 2, no. 2 (1987): 193.
Manwani, Harish. "Profit's Not Always the Point." *TED Talks* (2012).
Marshall, Kim. *Rethinking Teacher Supervision and Evaluation: How to Work Smart, Build Collaboration, and Close the Achievement Gap*. New York: John Wiley & Sons, 2013.
Martensen, Anne, and Jens J. Dahlgaard. "Integrating Business Excellence and Innovation Management: Developing Vision, Blueprint and Strategy for Innovation in Creative and Learning Organizations." *Total Quality Management* 10, no. 4–5 (1999): 627–35. doi: 10.1080/0954412997613.

McCullough, Charles. "What Matters Even More: Codifying the Public Purpose of Education to M." *Boston College Third World Law Journal*. Accessed May 17, 2015. http://lawdigitalcommons.bc.edu/twlj/vol27/iss1/3/.

McGregor, Douglas. "Theory X and Theory Y." *Organization Theory* (1960): 358–374.

Moran, Gwen. "5 Ways to Encourage Kids to Grow Up to Be Innovators." *Fast Company*. December 16, 2014. Accessed May 17, 2015. http://www.fastcompany.com/3039880/5-ways-to-encourage-kids-to-grow-up-to-be-innovators.

Mulligan, Michael. "The Three Most Important Questions You Can Ask Your Teenager." *The Huffington Post*. Accessed May 17, 2015. http://www.huffingtonpost.com/michael-mulligan/the-three-most-important-questions-you-can-ask-your-teenager_b_6173822.html.

Murata, Roberta. "What Does Team Teaching Mean? A Case Study of Interdisciplinary Teaming." *The Journal of Educational Research* 96, no. 2 (2002): 67–77. doi: 10.1080/00220670209598794.

National Commission on Excellence in Education (Gardner, D. P., Chair). "A Nation at Risk: The Imperative for Educational Reform." *The Elementary School Journal* 84, no. 2 (1983): 112. doi: 10.1086/461348.

New Tech Network. "Student Outcomes Report: Reimagining Teaching and Learning." 2014. Accessed March 2015. www.newtechnetwork.org/sites/default/files/resources/2014ntnstudentoutcomesreport1.pdf.

NPR Ed Team. "Kindergarten Entry Tests and More Education Predictions for 2015." *NPR*. Accessed May 17, 2015. http://www.npr.org/blogs/ed/2014/12/26/373268439/15-education-predictions-for-2015.

Oloruntegbe, Kunle Oke "Teachers' Involvement, Commitment and Innovativeness in Curriculum Development and Implementation." *Journal of Emerging Trends in Educational Research and Policy Studies* 2, no. 6 (2011): 443–449.

Ozturk, Ibrahim Hakki. "Teacher's Role and Autonomy in Instructional Planning: The Case of Secondary School History Teachers with Regard to the Preparation and Implementation of Annual Instructional Plans." *Educational Sciences: Theory and Practice* 12, no. 1 (2012): 295–299.

Padgett, Ray, Matt Hanks, Hector Silva, and Mark Satlof. "Embrace the Common Core." Intelligence² Debates. September 9, 2014. Accessed March 2015. http://intelligencesquaredus.org/debates/past-debates/item/1154-embrace-the-common-core.

Pennington, Kaitlin. "ESEA Waivers and Teacher-Evaluation Plans." *Name*. Accessed May 17, 2015. https://www.americanprogress.org/issues/education/report/2014/05/07/89121/esea-waivers-and-teacher-evaluation-plans/.

Petrie, Kirsten. "Enabling or Limiting: The Role of Pre-packaged Curriculum Resources in Shaping Teacher Learning." *Asia-Pacific Journal of Health, Sport and Physical Education* 3, no. 1 (2012): 17–34. doi: 10.1080/18377122.2012.666196.

Phillips, Joy. "Powerful Learning: Creating Learning Communities in Urban School Reform." *Journal of Curriculum and Supervision* 18, no. 3 (2003): 240–258.

Pianta, Robert C., Jay Belsky, Renate Houts, and Fred Morrison. "TEACHING: Opportunities to Learn in America's Elementary Classrooms." *Science* 315, no. 5820 (2007): 1795–1796. doi: 10.1126/science.1139719.

Pink, Daniel H. *Drive: The Surprising Truth about What Motivates Us*. New York: Riverhead Books, 2009.

Poole, Marybeth G., and Karen R. Okeafor. "The Effects of Teacher Efficacy and Interactions among Educators on Curriculum Implementation." *Journal of Curriculum and Supervision* 4, no. 2 (1989): 146–161.

Putnam, Robert. "Why You Should Care about Other People's Kids." *PBS*. Accessed May 17, 2015. http://www.pbs.org/newshour/making-sense/care-peoples-kids/.

Ravitch, Diane. *The Death and Life of the Great American School System: How Testing and Choice Are Undermining Education*. New York: Basic Books, 2010.

Ravitch, Diane. "Why I Cannot Support the Common Core Standards." *Diane Ravitch's Blog*. February 26, 2013. Accessed May 17, 2015. http://dianeravitch.net/2013/02/26/why-i-cannot-support-the-common-core-standards/.

Reeves, Douglas B. "High Performance in High Poverty Schools: 90/90/90 and Beyond." *Center for Performance Assessment* (2003): 1–20.

Reeves, Douglas B. *The Learning Leader: How to Focus School Improvement for Better Results*. Alexandria, VA: Association for Supervision and Curriculum Development, 2006.

Ricard, Matthieu. "The Habits of Happiness." *TED Talks* (2004).

Richardson, Connie. "The Mathematical Argument." *American Educational History Journal* 38 (2011): 27–288. Accessed March 2015. http://www.infoagepub.com/american-educational-history-journal.

Robb, Kathryn A., Alice E. Simon, and Jane Wardle. "Socioeconomic Disparities in Optimism and Pessimism." *International Journal of Behavioral Medicine* 16, no. 4 (2009): 331–38. doi: 10.1007/s12529-008-9018-0.

Robbins, Tony. "Why We Do What We Do." *TED Talks* (2006).

Robinson, Ken. "How Schools Kill Creativity." *TED Talks* (2006).

Robinson, Ken. "Changing Education Paradigms." *TED Talks* (2008).

Robinson, Ken. "Bring on the Learning Revolution!" *TED Talks* (2010).

Robinson, Ken. "How to Escape Education's Death Valley." *TED Talks* (2013).

Robinson, Ken. "What Graduation Speeches Should Say but Don't | TIME.com." Ideas What Graduation Speeches Should Say but Dont Comments. Accessed May 17, 2015. http://ideas.time.com/2013/05/21/what-graduation-speeches-should-really-say/.

Rothman, Robert. "A Common Core of Readiness." *Educational Leadership* 69, no. 7 (2012): 10–15.

Schaffhauser, Dian. "Teachers Mixed on Common Core, Support Blended Learning" THE Journal. Accessed May 17, 2015. http://thejournal.com/articles/2015/02/09/teachers-mixed-on-common-core-support-blended-learning.aspx.

Schleicher, Andreas. "Use Data to Build Better Schools." *TED Talks* (2012).

Schmoker, Michael J. *Focus: Elevating the Essentials to Radically Improve Student Learning*. Alexandria, VA: ASCD, 2011.

Schwartz, Katrina. "Unexpected Tools That Are Influencing the Future of Education." *MindShift*. Accessed May 17, 2015. http://blogs.kqed.org/mindshift/2015/01/unexpected-tools-that-are-influencing-the-future-of-education/.

Schwartz, Katrina. "How Integrating Arts into Other Subjects Makes Learning Come Alive." MindShift. Accessed May 17, 2015. http://blogs.kqed.org/mindshift/2015/01/how-integrating-arts-into-other-subjects-makes-learning-come-alive/.

Sethi, Kiran. "Kids, Take Charge." *TED Talks* (2009).

Shernoff, David J., Mihaly Csikszentmihalyi, Barbara Shneider, and Elisa Steele Shernoff. "Student Engagement in High School Classrooms from the Perspective of Flow Theory." *School Psychology Quarterly* 18, no. 2 (2003): 158–176. doi: 10.1521/scpq.18.2.158.21860.

Siller, Anna. "Richer School Districts in 23 States Are Receiving More Local Funding than Their Poorer Counterparts." *PBS*. Accessed May 17, 2015. http://www.pbs.org/newshour/rundown/23-states-richer-school-districts-receive-local-funds-poor/.

Singh, Maavi. "Why Emotional Learning May Be as Important as the ABCs." *NPR*. Accessed May 17, 2015. http://www.npr.org/blogs/ed/2014/12/31/356187871/why-emotional-literacy-may-be-as-important-as-learning-the-a-b-c-s.

Sinek, Simon. "How Great Leaders Inspire Action. Simon Sinek." *TED Talks* (2009).

Sinek, Simon. *Start with Why: How Great Leaders Inspire Everyone to Take Action*. New York: Portfolio, 2009.

Slack, Kristen Shook, Jane L. Holl, Maria Mcdaniel, Joan Yoo, and Kerry Bolger. "Understanding the Risks of Child Neglect: An Exploration of Poverty and Parenting Characteristics." *Child Maltreatment: A Collection of Readings*, 2012, 182–201. doi: 10.4135/9781452230689.n12.

Spiegel, Alix. "Teachers' Expectations Can Influence How Students Perform." *NPR*. Accessed May 17, 2015. http://www.npr.org/blogs/health/2012/09/18/161159263/teachers-expectations-can-influence-how-students-perform.

Spring, Joel. American Education (14th ed.). New York: McGraw-Hill, 2008.

Starecheski, Laura. "A Sheriff and a Doctor Team Up to Map Childhood Trauma." *NPR*. Accessed May 17, 2015. http://www.npr.org/blogs/health/2015/03/10/377566905/a-sheriff-and-a-doctor-team-up-to-map-childhood-trauma.

Starnes, Bobby Ann. "Change, Sputnik, and Fast Food." *Phi Delta Kappan* 92, no. 7 (2011): 72–73.

Stinson, Anne D'Antonio, William Chandler, M. Epps, and Melissa Frieberg. "Multi-Context Use of Language: Toward Effective Thinking and Planning for Curriculum." *Mid-Western Educational Researcher* 19, no. 4 (2006): 24–29, 73. doi: 10.1177/003172171109200717.

St. John, Richard. "8 Secrets of Success." *TED Talks* (2005).

Strauss, Valerie. "School Superintendent Writes 'Warning' Letter on PARCC Common Core Test." *Washington Post*. Accessed May 17, 2015. http://www.washingtonpost.com/blogs/answer-sheet/wp/2015/01/26/school-superintendent-writes-warning-letter-on-parcc-common-core-test/.

Strauss, Valerie. "What If Finland's Great Teachers Taught in U.S. Schools?" *Washington Post*. Accessed May 17, 2015. http://www.washingtonpost.com/blogs/answer-sheet/wp/2013/05/15/what-if-finlands-great-teachers-taught-in-u-s-schools-not-what-you-think/.

Streep, Meryl. *School: The Story of American Public Education*. Edited by Sarah Mondale, and Sarah B. Patton. Boston: Beacon Press, 2002.

The Curricular Review Group. *A Curriculum for Excellence*. Edinburgh: Scottish Executive, 2004.

Thompson, Derek. "Why Gloomy Pundits and Politicians Are Wrong about America's Education System." *The Atlantic*, January 22, 2013. Accessed May 17, 2015. http://www.theatlantic.com/business/archive/2013/01/

why-gloomy-pundits-and-politicians-are-wrong-about-americas-education-system/267278/.
Turner, Julianne C., A. Christensen, Hayal Zeynep Kackar-Cam, Michael Trucano, and Sara M. Fulmer. "Enhancing Students' Engagement: Report of a 3-Year Intervention with Middle School Teachers." *American Educational Research Journal* 51, no. 6 (2014): 1195–1226. doi: 10.3102/0002831214532515.
Walsch, Neale Donald. *When Everything Changes, Change Everything: In a Time of Turmoil, a Pathway to Peace*. Hachette UK, 2010.
Walters, Garrison. "Dump Management 'Science,' and Change Learning Attitudes." *Education Week* 34, no. 19 (2015): 25–27. http://www.edweek.org.
Warner, John. "Education Reformers Don't Know What 'College Ready' Means." Accessed May 17, 2015. https://www.insidehighered.com/blogs/just-visiting/education-reformers-dont-know-what-college-ready-means.
Watkins, Debbie, and William Allan Kritsonis. "Developing and Designing an Effective School Curriculum: Enhancing Student Achievement Based on an Integrated Curriculum Model and the Ways of Knowing through the Realms of Meaning." *Focus on Colleges, Universities & Schools* 6. no. 1 (December 2011): 1.
Webb, L. Dean. *The History of American Education: A Great American Experiment*. Upper Saddle River, NJ: Pearson/Merrill/Prentice Hall, 2006.
Wert, Allison. "5 Things Your Teachers Want You to Know." Accessed May 17, 2015. http://www.frontlinek12.com/Pages/Blog/5_Things_Your_Teachers_Want_You_To_Know.html.
Willis, Judy. *Research-based Strategies to Ignite Student Learning: Insights from a Neurologist and Classroom Teacher*. Alexandria, VA: Association for Supervision and Curriculum Development, 2006.
Wiseman, Paul. "Firms Seek Grads Who Can Think Fast, Work in Teams." *Star Tribune*. Accessed May 17, 2015. http://www.startribune.com/business/212770791.html.
Wolfram, Conrad. "Teaching Kids Real Math with Computers." *TED Talks* (2010).
Yazzie-Mintz, Ethan. *Voices of Students on Engagement: A Report on the 2006 High School Survey of Student Engagement*. Center for Evaluation and Education Policy, Indiana University (2007).
Zhao, Yong. "Are We Fixing the Wrong Things?" *Educational Leadership* 63, no. 8 (2006): 28–31.
Zhbanova, Ksenia S., Audrey C. Rule, Sarah E. Montgomery, and Lynn E. Nielsen. "Defining the Difference: Comparing Integrated and Traditional Single-Subject Lessons." *Early Childhood Education Journal* 38, no. 4 (2010): 251–258. doi: 10.1007/s10643-010-0405-1.
Zimbardo, Philip G. "The Psychology of Evil." *Eye on Psi Chi* (2000): 16–19.

About the Author

 **Amy Fast**, EdD is an instructional coach at both the elementary and secondary level for the McMinnville School District in McMinnville, Oregon. As an instructional coach, her role is to lead professional development in the district, model effective instruction for teachers, and observe teachers to provide feedback for improvement. Prior to instructional coaching, Amy was a classroom teacher for ten years with experience in both fourth and fifth grades. As a teacher, Amy received much recognition from school and district leaders for her students' monumental achievement and growth in her classroom. In 2015, Amy received her doctorate in educational leadership from George Fox University in Newberg, Oregon.